This book is full of living your royal heart. The Lord Himself dwells within pages. Time and time again Teresa's insights brought Jolene and me into living encounters which deeply matured our understanding of how to relate to God and receive from Him. Much of the content proved corrective, but in the same stunning way that glasses provide corrective vision. The complexities of prayer become transformed into simple and life-giving gateways to see Christ's beauty and justice manifested in your world. An amazing work!

Jon & Jolene Hamill--Cofounders,
Lamplighter Ministries
Washington DC

Teresa Cantrell is not only an anointed intercessor, she is a gifted author. She reminds us that we see only a small framework through a dimly lit tunnel. Our Creator King sees the big picture. He challenges us through His Holy Spirit to rest in His love. Trust in His power and wisdom. Anticipate His grace and deliverance. His answers may seem delayed on our schedule, but He will certainly answer without delay on His sovereign timetable. Drawing from personal experience, strong scriptural foundations, and practical prayer tools, Teresa will inspire you to move from tunnel vision to divine perspective, ashes to beauty, mourning to joy, and Groaning to Glory!

Kay Horner--Executive Director
Awakening America Alliance
&
The Helper Connection
Cleveland, Tennessee

I believe that God is raising up a generation of intercessors. People who have a passion to experience breakthroughs in prayer. Teresa Cantrell is a trusted guide. She has devoted her life to prayer and helping others experience the same freedom and joy. Regardless how long you have walked with Jesus, the words in these pages will not only help you be more effective in prayer, but more importantly they will help you know the heart of God.

Kevin Queen--Lead Pastor, Cross Point Church Nashville, Tennessee

---

This book on prayer has the ring of a classic. Teresa uses her vivid life experiences, enlightened by Scripture — with quotes from key devotional writers — to give new insight into the essential, privileged ministry of prayer.

Ruth Trippy--Award-winning Author of The Soul of the Rose

This is a very powerful and wonderful book! Teresa reveals tools that enable people to grow in their relationship with Jesus Christ, but also tools for unleashing the "Christ within them, the hope of glory" through a dynamic prayer life. This is a great resource for small groups!"

Randy Tindall--Small Groups Pastor, Business Executive Retired Army Officer

From Groans to Glory provides foundational truth for every believer seeking to learn about their identity, as an intercessor in the Kingdom of God. The personal testimonies, revelatory insights and heartfelt wisdom are beautifully woven together, creating a unique tapestry that depicts the destiny and authority God planned for each of us from the beginning of time.
Lynn Alderson-- Co-Founder
Kingdom Authority Ministries, Inc.

Teresa is a true prayer warrior who shares tried and proven principles for both personal and corporate prayer that are uplifting and transformational. Leading corporate prayer is a gift and a necessity for the days head. Teresa is a joy to work with in encouraging and enhancing prayer across the state of Georgia.
David Franklin-- Georgia State Coordinator
National Day of Prayer Task Force

You hold a valuable book in your hands. This book is birthed by a beautiful and seasoned warrior of the faith, my good friend Teresa Cantrell. As you read it, you will be swept up in the powerful flow of His Spirit as Teresa brings truth about who the Father is and how He engages His children in prayer and conversations on earth, even in the marketplace! Teresa majestically weaves her tender stories of her family, particularly her dad, into the tools and practices of daily prayer and intercession to show us how to "pray through" to get the break through. You will be both touched and inspired to go deeper in prayer with our heavenly Father.
Bill Blane--New Gates

From Groans To Glory

Keys To Breakthrough Prayer

Teresa Hinton Cantrell

ENTEGRITY
CHOICE PUBLISHING

Entegrity Choice Publishing
PO Box 453
Powder Springs, GA 30127
info@entegritypublishing.com │ 770.727.6517

ISBN: 978-0-9991780-9-6

Library of Congress Control Number:
2018905237

Printed in the United States of America

Dedication

This book is lovingly dedicated to my father, Dr. Leonard Hinton. My earliest memories as a child are of my father kneeling in prayer by our turquoise tweed sofa with an open and heavily underlined Bible. As our gentle God would have it, I have spent the last few months serving Dad with the support of Hospice care. Much of the book you are about to read was written on the very same sofa (although re-covered in a lovely but still outdated floral.)

This year I have seen an unusual number of posts from dear friends who have released loved ones into the arms of Jesus. My own heart was breaking as I watched my beloved Daddy struggling to recuperate from heart surgery just after Christmas, 2016. On February 22, 2017, we brought him home with hospice care, but not before a tender moment together at the rehab facility.

Just before we had packed up and prepared to go home, Dad and I sat in his room at the healthcare facility and began to pray. As the presence of God filled the room I was reminded of another transition in 2 Kings 2:9.

"After they had crossed over, Elijah said to Elisha, 'Tell me what I can do for you before I am taken from you.' So, Elisha answered, 'Please let there be a double portion of your spirit on me.'" I heard God say in my spirit, "I know you are grieving and hurting over this transition, but be encouraged and see what I am doing! I have heard every prayer from every generation, and this is the day, this is the year, this is the time, that I am answering in double portion blessing. Watch and pray with bold expectation."

I began to pray that Dad's zeal for Christ, his love of Scripture, his love of people, and his desire that all people know his Savior would be given double to his children, grandchildren, great grandchildren, and spiritual children. I prayed that throughout the whole Church, the prayers of one generation would be answered and multiplied by the next generation.

One of Dad's favorite scriptures was Colossians 1:27, "Christ in you, the hope of glory." I believe this is a unique year when God is restoring His glory to broken people, hurting families and a divided America. This is the year of double portion blessing, and these special "homecomings" mark the beginning of a new outpouring of His Spirit.

As we prayed and worshipped, Dad raised both hands fully extended, eyes closed and face upturned. This season had been rough. His body was weakened throughout each day and his mind often confused, but his spirit? His spirit was vibrant, fresh, free and confident in his Jesus. I am forever grateful for the rich heritage of love and for godly earthly parents that enriched and revealed a sweet perspective of my loving and compassionate heavenly Father. Dad was taken up into glory on March 29, 2017. I miss you dearly and love you forever, Daddy.

DR. LEONARD O. HINTON, JR.

July 27, 1931-March 29, 2017

Pictured with author, daughter Teresa Hinton Cantrell

Acknowledgement

Special thanks to my niece Sara Cantrell, for the use of her beautiful painting on the cover. Sara earned a Bachelor of Arts with concentration in Painting and Drawing, from Anderson University, 2018. May God's creative touch continue to flow through your gifted and anointed hands!

With Great Gratitude

I am grateful for my husband Mike, the love of my youth, my steady rock, my best friend and the engineer who balances my artsy, passionate boldness.

♥

My precious adult children who taught me about God's heart and continue to bless me with teachable spirits, courage and beautiful destinies unfolding.

♥

My mother, Joanne J. Hinton, who prays for me daily and models consistent unconditional love and mercy.

♥

My wise and gentle sister Patti, sister-in-law Lori, life-long friend Julie and so many dear friends and prayer partners. Each of you holds a tender place in my heart as we have shared a glimpse of God's glory in our answered prayers.

♥

Mentors, Pastors, Apostles and Prophets who have spoken into my life and helped me connect the dots of my uniquely crafted journey so that I can share it with you.

Contents

Introduction

"May the LORD God, the God of Israel,
be praised, who alone does wonders. May His glorious
name be praised forever; the whole earth
is filled with His GLORY."
Psalm 72:18-19

As 2017 dawned, a heightened expectation filled the air. The United States of America had just endured one of the most brutal and controversial presidential elections in the history of our young republic. There had emerged a clear and distinct schism in American ideology and attitudes. Both sides, liberal progressives and conservative patriots, thought the other side incredibly shortsighted and misguided.

The Church as a whole seemed equally divided on many issues. While some struggled with apathy, embarrassment, anger, and fear, a remnant began to emerge that could see things from a different perspective. Prophetic voices began to unite with dreams, visions, and words that explained a spiritual shift that was taking place. Some described it as a conflict of thrones. (See posts from Jon Hamill of Lamplighter Ministry-jonandjolene.us). Many saw that the incredibly unusual turn of events in the natural was actually a reflection of very real and powerful battles in the spiritual realm.

For those of us who have been interceding for America and her people for decades, the changes stirring in the air ignited fresh hope. We knew nothing short of an awakening and outpouring of the Holy Spirit could begin to heal our land. We have been on our knees, both in private closets and in corporate gatherings small and large for over 30 years. In the months preceding the 2016 election, there were more prayer conference calls, national calls to prayer and fasting, and fervent intercession than I have ever seen in my life. Thousands of believers united across race, denomination, location, education, and economics to cry out for a turnaround in our Nation.

As I completed 40 days of prayer and a "Daniel" fast on election day, a quiet confidence and "knowing" settled into my Spirit. Somehow, I knew God had heard the prayers of saints throughout generations past and present and He was showing mercy to His children once again. This positive and hopeful outlook was not accidental or naive. It has developed from years of seeking to understand the bold and powerful promises of God that are lived out and applied to reality as we experience it. Whether in personal intercession for my children, family and friends or in corporate intercession for a ministry, city or nation, I have learned so much from the best and wisest Teacher.

This upbeat, optimistic attitude arises from true intercession. The same peace of "knowing" that I experienced while praying for our nation has occurred while praying with friends and family. Whether a dear friend whose sister had just been diagnosed with inoperable brain tumors or my friend whose estranged daughter had been arrested and charged with serious felony charges, prayer shifts the attitude of our hearts.

> **In the midst of dire circumstances, God's perspective and presence push back despair.**

In the midst of dire circumstances, God's perspective and presence, His magnificent Glory arose to push back despair and hopelessness and gloom.

In this book, I pray that the Holy Spirit uses my pen and personal journey to bring you to a new place of overcoming, confident, and joyful living. Intercession is the most amazing and life-changing gift we can offer our loved ones. Rooted in relationship with a Righteous Judge and intimacy with a Passionate Lover, our prayers take on new vibrancy, specificity, purpose, and power.

The result is an old-fashioned word becomes an explosive new reality- GLORY!

We are living in unprecedented days. The media fuels fear by twisting and distorting coverage, inundating us with bad news and even "fake" news. But Christ has made it possible to view the reality of life from God's perspective. He has reconciled us to a Holy God, invites us into the glory and truth found in His presence and *that* is really "good news!"

A lifestyle of abiding prayer holds the key. Christ has already overcome the world and given us authority to act on His behalf. It is possible to cross over from fear to faith. Invite the Holy Spirit to teach, comfort and lead you; ushering you into the powerful mystery of "Christ in you, the hope of glory!"

1

I Will Pray for You!

In the midst of life's most difficult situations, we often hear a common response. *"I will pray for you."* What typically becomes of that promise? Forgotten as we whisk forward toward a busy day? Even when we do remember to pray, is it anything deeper than a cursory plea asking the Lord to please help our friend in their tough time? If we linger in prayer, do we tend to plead for a change in circumstances, telling God how to mend the situation, all the while ending our prayer time still shouldering a burden and heaviness of heart?

This book has been birthed in a life journey of learning how to "pray through" a situation until God's perspective brings hope and life. Just as the labor of child birth brings groans of pain before the glory of new birth, fervent prevailing prayer also balances on this continuum. Too often we stay in the gloom and pain of the groaning stage when God longs for us to press in until we break through into His glory. We may not "see" the change that is taking place, but God assures us there is an "unseen" shift that occurs when we pray in alignment with Him, and it brings great joy.

Just a few months ago, our family found ourselves in a difficult situation. After graduation from college, our son had experienced repeated job loss. He had moved to a different city to try and start over and met a young lady there whom he desired to marry. He had just been let go from yet another employer who he thought held promise for a rewarding career. She was not employed either, and we advised a delay in the marriage until there was more financial and emotional stability. They chose to get married anyway, hoping things would change.

Instead of improving, bills piled up, stress escalated, communication was broken, and fear and anxiety bound them, incapacitating any forward movement or initiative to change. A psychiatrist prescribed medication that, while providing temporary emotional relief, exacerbated the problem leading to sleep-filled, groggy days. Our advice was received as criticism, and the result was hopeless isolation with distorted thinking and a lack of real solutions. Migraines and nausea developed, further limiting healthy change, and eviction from their apartment was eminent. It seemed these latest, devastating circumstances merely confirmed his feeling that "Everything was hard for him, but easy for everybody else." A victim mentality colored every thought.

During a time of prayer one morning I was struck by a comment from Moses:

> *"Moses told this to the Israelites, but they did not listen to him because of their broken spirit and hard labor." Exodus 6:9*

The preceding verses in Chapter 6 are full of the promises of God concerning Israel's freedom and future. God said,

- I will let them **know** My name in a personal way as never before.

- I will **remember** and keep my covenant and promises to them.

- I will **deliver** them from the hard labor.

- I will **free** them from what enslaves.

- I will **redeem** them with outstretched arm and **judge** their oppressors.

- I will **take** them as My people.

- They will **know** Me.

- I will **bring** them to the land I promised.

All of these assurances were heard and understood by Moses, the intercessor, but when he tried to comfort the people and advise or lead them in the next steps, they did not listen. They could not move forward due to their broken spirit from the "hard" labor of life. This was exactly how I felt about my son's situation! I knew the promises of God for him but could not get him to see them for himself and act on them. It broke my heart to see him hurting so much.

The way God instructed Moses to respond to this dire situation is a powerful example for us. Moses and Aaron together declared the purpose, power, and intentions of God to the people. But when the people were unable to respond and believe for themselves, God said to go tell Pharaoh to let the Israelites go! The intercessor was instructed to deal with the root cause of the bondage and declare the purposes and power of God over the enemy.

Moses stood in the gap between the reality of God's promises in the heavens and the enemies attempts to thwart the experience of that reality on earth for a people too broken in spirit to stand for themselves.

This is exactly what we must do when praying for others. Rather than just pleading for earthly circumstances to change, we seek to understand the heart of the Father for the situation and address any hindrance to the experience of that destiny.

My son and his wife were too broken in spirit to do the next right thing. They were so overwhelmed by the hard labor of life that they couldn't see the promises of God for themselves. Our family stood in the gap and began to declare the promises of God and deal with the enemy on behalf of our loved ones. I personally spent hours in worship and prayer on my knees. God gave me dreams and scripture to better understand what was going on in the spiritual realm. We organized a family intervention and made an unexpected visit to their apartment. I recruited an army of intercessors to stand with us in the spiritual battle.

Every human is beautifully, uniquely, amazingly created in the image of God. In the following chapters, we will delve into the impact of free will, choices, the original intent of our relationship with our Creator, and how Christ has restored the possibility of living in that original relationship. Most important, on what authority can someone stand in the gap or intercede for another person? Can we really expect change to result?

Does God intervene, overriding the natural cause and effect of choices and behavior? Sometimes. Again, with Moses as our example, the children of Israel exhibited defiant behavior by creating a golden calf to worship when God's expected answer was delayed. (Exodus 32) Rightfully, Holy God was ready to destroy every one of them for their rebellious, idolatrous behavior, but Moses interceded. He reminded God of His covenant promises and asked for mercy. ***And God relented***. The prayers of Moses certainly changed the outcome for an entire nation.

During a recent gathering of intercessors at Stone Mountain Georgia, we cried out to God, repenting of the ugly sin of racism that divides our city and state. The leader read from Joel 2:12-14, a scriptural example where God used disaster as a part of His plan to heal and restore.

We gathered, first declaring and worshipping God's attributes, agreeing with the prophet that, "He is gracious and compassionate, slow to anger, rich in faithful love, and **relents** from sending disaster." Like my prayer for a hurting son and Moses' prayer for a wayward people, we then asked, "Who knows? He may turn and **relent** and leave a blessing behind Him…"

Pain and suffering originate from various sources. My own journey has shown me that the greatest benefit from pressing through in prayer is more than just changing circumstances - it is knowing God Himself more fully.

> *"Come, let us return to the LORD, for He has torn us but He will heal us; He has wounded us, and He will bind up our wounds. Let us strive to know the LORD." Hosea 6:1,3a*

This book delves into both the foundation of breakthrough prayer and the application of that prayer. At the end of each chapter I have written a sample prayer to be read aloud: based on scripture, it provides an example of how to "pray in" a truth or promise that God reveals in His Word.

Precious Jesus,

I worship You as Intercessor. All powers are under Your authority, so I know that what You say will be done. Your Holy Spirit also knows the heart of the Father in this matter and is interceding on our behalf beyond human words. I desire for my words to be in agreement with Your plans and purposes, and I ask for knowledge to know how to pray to release those plans into action.

Jesus, Your finished work on the cross makes it possible for an intimate relationship with Holy God to be restored. Based on this covenant, I ask today that the deliverance, redemption, and freedom that You already paid for become a reality to my loved one. Because they are broken in spirit from hard labor, I am asking that you defend them against their adversary, rebuke the effectiveness of the enemy's schemes against them, and show me how to fight for them.

You have not given us a spirit of fear but of power, love, and sound mind. Reveal truth and strengthen our hearts to act on the promises You have given us. Amen.

Exodus 6:2-11, Romans 8, 2 Corinthians 5:21, Ephesians 1:20-23, 2 Timothy 1:7

2

A Time to Groan

Once upon a time, all that mankind knew was "good." It was before the deadly ingestion of the fruit from the tree of the knowledge of good...and evil. In the garden, there was open, spontaneous, refreshing dialog. Adam and Eve walked and talked with God, listened and responded. It is easy to imagine God's glory filling the earth then- before the defiant choice *not* to believe God.

Surely there was an awe at their Creator's knowledge and wise answers to their constant barrage of questions and observations. Humility and submission came easily as every single experience confirmed their view that this Creator, their God, was faithful, kind, trustworthy, and true. Before the consequence of sin that resulted in the groaning of labor and evil, there was glory.

Today our return to this place of intimate conversation in the garden is prayer. Prayer is a simple word that is unfortunately interchanged too often with petition or request, but it is so much more! Prayer involves the fullness of two-way communication in intimate relationship. It involves responding with adoration of His attributes, seeking deeper understanding when questions arise, and sometimes requesting resources.

Prayer can certainly be introspective and focused on personal needs and change. But the moment the second human was added to the garden, the God-conversation expanded to advocating for the needs of another person. Any time we are standing in the gap for another person or group, it is called *intercession*.

Effective and powerful intercession involves listening to the heart of God in heaven, then speaking it on earth.

Like the term prayer, intercession has been too often narrowed to mean just petition on behalf of another person. In reality, like the conversation initiated in the garden, intercession involves listening and responding. Hearing and speaking God's perspective is *prophetic intercession*.

The most effective and powerful intercession necessarily involves listening to the perspective and heart of God in heaven, then speaking it on earth.

He alone knows the plans He has for our friends and the spiritual barriers that are hindering the fulfillment of those plans. Amazingly, He has expressed His willingness and desire to share and reveal that perspective!

One of the most effective and fervent intercessors of recent time was the Welsh miner, Rees Howells (1879-1950). His biography is filled with experience-chiseled wisdom. He explains, "Perhaps believers in general have regarded intercession as just some form of rather intensified prayer. It is, so long as there is great emphasis on the word 'intensified'; for there are three things to be seen in an intercessor, which are not necessarily found in ordinary prayer: identification, agony, and authority." [1]

This principle is so foundational to effective intercession that it deserves a fuller explanation in Howells' own words. "The identification of the intercessor with the ones for whom he intercedes is perfectly seen in the Savior. Of Him it was said that He poured out his soul unto death; and He was numbered with the transgressors; and He bore the sin of many, and made *intercession* for the transgressors... Identification is thus the first law of the intercessor. He pleads effectively because he gives his life for those he pleads for; he is their genuine representative... " [2]

Howells continues, "But intercession is more than the Spirit sharing His groaning with us, and living His life of sacrifice for the world through us. It is the Spirit gaining His ends of abundant grace. If the intercessor knows identification and agony, he also knows authority. But identification so identifies the intercessor with the sufferer that it gives him a prevailing place with God. He moves God." [3]

If you have really followed through on a promise to pray for someone, it is probable that you have felt the pain and burden they carry. This is particularly true when you have personally experienced a similar trial. For instance, when a mother calls me because her child has been arrested for drug use and is facing a judge tomorrow, I feel the agony of their unknown future. I feel the heart-wrenching fear of hardened criminals interacting with, deceiving, and influencing her vulnerable child. I grieve

> **Much groaning is over loss of human comfort rather than grief over dishonoring God.**

over the consequences, lost opportunity, and hard path the present choices present. My friend needs to know I understand her pain and share her agony. I've received that call from a jail phone myself.

But the beauty of identification is that groaning and agony is not where we stay. Using the earned authority God has crowned us with, we begin to declare God's desire to bring good out of the enemy's attack of evil. We declare destruction will not prevail but instead God's destiny will be released. We ask for protection, provision, and divine intervention- and believe it is done.

There is a groaning that God honors and values. It is the identification with the holiness of His character and anguish over the abomination of idolatry. How much of our groaning is over the loss of human comfort or convenience rather that a grief over the disrespect and dishonoring of God Himself?

The original glorious atmosphere in the garden brought pleasure to God and man. The rebellious choice of sin brought devastating consequence to man, but it also broke God's heart.

In the vision experienced by Ezekiel recorded in chapter 9 he says,

> *"Then the glory of the God of Israel rose from above the cherubim where it had been, to the threshold of the temple. He called to the man clothed in linen with the writing equipment at his side. 'Pass throughout the city of Jerusalem,' the LORD said to him, 'and put a mark on the foreheads of the men who sigh and groan over all the abominations committed in it.'" Ezekiel 9:3-4*

Travail is modeled by Christ in Gethsemane. There is a place for wrestling. There is a time to sigh and groan.

The word translated "mark" in the passage above is the Hebrew letter "taw", the name of the final letter in the Hebrew alphabet. In ancient Hebrew the "taw" was shaped like an X or "cross." Each one who received this mark would be spared. Christian interpreters view this mark as a type of Christ (Revelation 7:3, 9:4).

The consistency of God's redemptive plan from Genesis to Revelation never ceases to amaze me! In Ezekiel God revealed a very descriptive image of His glory lingering at the threshold of the temple. He notices and "marks" those who are groaning with remorse over the sin and brokenness in their city.

There is an identification with the holiness of our Father and the offer of life for His children that causes us to groan when it is not experienced. But staying there is like returning to the garden *after* the fall instead of *before* the fall! Christ's resurrection brought victory, life, and the hope of returning to "original glory!"

Glorious Father,

Thank You for creating such a colorful, exciting, and glorious world for us to live in. You are the source of every good and perfect gift! There is so much beauty and delight in the life You designed.

Forgive us, Lord, for the rebellious choices and unbelief that cause such brokenness and destruction within Your world. We are eternally grateful that You initiated a plan of redemption from the very beginning that could restore us back to relationship with You and Your glory.

As I pray, please give me eyes to see, ears to hear, and a heart to understand Your ways. Break my heart over what breaks Yours and allow me to be a part of the restoration solution. God, I truly want to return to the glory of the garden where I can linger in Your presence. I know that every need I have and every need I intercede for is fully met in who You are! I strive to press on to know you deeper every day of my life. I love You, Triune God! Amen.

James 1:17, John 3:16-18, Ezekiel 9:3-4
Revelation 7:3, Hosea 6:1-3, Romans 3:9-26

3

A Good Father

My sweet Daddy's tired blue eyes sparkled as he looked into mine. "Just think about it Teresa," he said, "Five words: 'In the beginning God created...'" His 85-year-old body had just been through excruciating surgery. Shortly after the whole family gathered for Christmas 2016, Dad went in for heart bypass surgery. During the process, they also discovered a cancerous tumor lurking in his bladder, perhaps one more explanation for his absolute lack of appetite and ongoing exhaustion. The hospital stay that was supposed to be 4 days turned into 10, and rehab that was supposed to be several weeks turned into a month. It was in this small nursing home room, surrounded by the aging and ailing, seated in his wheelchair that he made this profound statement.

Although New Year's Day arrived with me sleeping in a hospital recliner in ICU and January was a blur, I treasured the extended time spent with this remarkable saint. His body was slowly succumbing to the effects of aging, but his mind, although still struggling with the challenge of short term memory and comprehension, percolated with wonder and awe. He was amazed at the way the body functions and gave his Creator all the credit. Inspired by the nurses' knowledge, care, and explanations of medicine and treatment plans, he constantly thanked them and told them they were doing a great job.

Dad loved listening to my stories of prayer at the Capitol, updates on friends and family and even my theological and philosophical commentary on the news we were watching on TV. It was during these conversations that he mentioned more than once, "Just think about those five words, 'In the beginning God created.'" I quickly learned that while his body and mind were weakened with age, his spirit was still fully alive and being used by Holy Spirit to drop precious nuggets of value into my own spirit. His awe at the intricacy and beauty of God's creation-- both macro and micro, echoes my own wonder and establishes the foundational principles for understanding who we are created to be and our divine purpose.

It was during these hours of lingering in my earthly father's presence that my heavenly Father asked me to write down and share some of the insights He had taught me through the years about meaningful and effective conversation with Him. Prayer. Specifically, prayer on behalf of other individuals, groups, and regions. It is in His heart to bring us into a place of overcoming glory of His perspective.

God never intended a one-way conversation during which we list our problems and pain without listening to the answers and solutions from His perspective.

In today's fast-paced world of information and technology, there is no shortage of opinions as to who we are and why we are here. But when we roll back the slick media messages and escalating expectations, all the way to Genesis, there is a simple yet profound original intent of our Creator. Genesis 1:26 begins, **"Let Us make man in Our Image."** The "Us" reveals that God already eternally existed in Triune mystery. The revelation continues to unfold throughout the entirety of Scripture, and multiple names reflect multiple divine traits and characteristics. Deuteronomy 6:4 states, **"The LORD our God, the LORD is One."** The Hebrew root word "echad" used for "One" in this passage suggests unified

> **God never intended a one-way conversation where we list our problems without listening to His perspective.**

in purpose as one, like husband and wife becoming "one" flesh (Genesis 2:24), not simply the number one.

We see that Father, Son, and Spirit are One God, yet connected relationally to each other. Created in that image, we also carry multiple roles in one person. I am mother, daughter, wife, and sister. I relate in different ways not only to my human family but to my Creator.

> **If prayer is a conversation with God, the specific appeal varies on the relationship with which we approach Him.**

Because God has invited us into relationship with Him, our prayer is a two-way conversation which develops that relationship. It involves both speaking and listening. Listening is so important to knowing the thoughts and plans of God and understanding the hindrances to those plans. Hearing God's perspective is a key difference between pleading our desires rather than proclaiming His intentions. This is the basic meaning of "prophetic" intercession- hearing, praying, and declaring God's heart.

If prayer is a conversation with God, the specific appeal and conversation varies on the relationship with which we approach Him.

I cry out to Him as Abba Father when I am addressing personal needs. I address Him as Adonai, my Lord, when I seek to know how I can serve Him. I stand in rapt attention as I listen for strategy for war from the Lord of Hosts. I linger in His presence, eyes locked in His loving gaze as I savor the embrace of my Beloved. Understanding our relational identity is crucial as we mature in prayer and intercession. As with any dear one that we love, time spent together and doing things together develops intimacy.

The first words from our mouths in prayer should be adoration, reverence, and awe that the Sovereign, All-powerful, All-knowing Eternal Almighty God would invite us into a relationship! This humble entrance into His presence is the essence of worship.

Worship is the most effective approach to moving us from anxious, earth-bound pleading to confident, victorious governance from a heavenly perspective.

Worship moves us from anxious pleading to victorious governance.

Worry cannot coexist with worship. Ruth Heflin remarks on the conversation between Jesus and the woman at the well in Samaria. "She asked Him many questions. He gave her one of the greatest revelations. It shows what God wants. He is seeking worshippers. If you want to live in the glory realm, you must be a worshipper. 'The Father seeks such to worship Him.' That is what He wants from the earth."[4]

Scripture is brimming with revelation of Who God is for us. Sylvia Gunter has prepared incredibly effective tools to use in the ministry of intercession. The following is a partial list from her material, "The I AM...For Our Every Need." [5]

HE IS...............FOR OUR NEEDS

Abba Father	when we need fathering
All sufficient	in our hardest situations
Answer	for uncertainty and questions
Cleansing	for defilement and shame
Defender	when we are under attack
Faithful Friend	when friends fail us
Healer	for woundedness, rejection, physical sickness
Joy	when we are depressed
Provider	for every financial need
Strong	when we are weak
Rest	when we are tired and can't go on
Wisdom	for hard choices
Truth	when we have been lied to

Worship shifts our perspective from our need to the One who is the solution to all things. Rather than dwelling on the circumstances we see on earth, we are able to set our minds on the reality of the unseen as it is in heaven. As we worship the names and attributes of God, the needs we bring before the throne are met by the King Himself.

Heavenly Father,

I am humbled by your kind invitation to enter into relationship with You! You are such a good, good Father! I am seated with Christ in heavenly places and given the authority of a daughter of the King! I long to mature into the fullness of Christ and accomplish the Kingdom purposes designed for me. Help me move past childish, self-centered, earth-bound requests.

As Jesus taught me to pray, I want to be a part of Your Kingdom coming on earth as it already is in Heaven. I trust You for the daily physical needs. Uproot any unforgiveness or bitterness in my heart that is leading to unhealthy thinking and actions. You are the great "I AM" that meets every need. I worship and exalt the beauty of who You are!

I love Your passion! I lift my loved ones before You and long for them to also know You intimately and fully. Thank you for running toward us with open arms! Please draw my loved one to return to Your arms. Amen.

Matthew 6:9-13, Ephesians 2:6, Romans 8:29
Psalm 73:16-17, Luke 15:20, Exodus 3:14, John 8:58

4

Glory-Atmosphere of Heaven

I always loved visiting Dad's house. He had shelves and shelves of books, every award that any family member had received, a collection of ball caps from every place he had visited, slides, photos, LP albums, cassettes and videos galore! Although a little (OK a lot) cluttered, he loved life and treasured memories through a gazillion keepsakes.

The atmosphere in the Hinton home was filled with his smile and huge personality. You could say his "presence" was manifest there. In trying to understand the term "glory," it helps to imagine Heaven as the home of God, filled with all the things He loves and treasures that express who He is.

It is nothing short of amazing that Eternal God, omnipresent, omnipotent, and omniscient, would create a being "in His image." What does the "Original" look like from which He created this "Image?" How accurate is the representation He created? How is it limited?

Perhaps the most inclusive word that describes God's attributes and existence is **Glory**. From the Latin Gloria, the word includes reference to one's fame or renown. It is also used to describe the external manifestation of God's being and presence as perceived by humans.

Relationship with the Father has been restored by Christ and activated by the Spirit, allowing heavenly glory on earth.

Our glimpse into the Creation story reveals that God possessed Glory prior to and separate from any manifestation of it. Yet, He invited man to experience it. You may have heard the hopeless phrase, "My prayers just don't get past the ceiling!" Truly there is a physical chasm between heaven and earth, but the amazing truth is that God has provided the means to transcend the gap.

Our original relationship with the Father has been restored by the sacrifice of Christ and is activated by the indwelling Spirit so that we can partake of the glorious atmosphere of heaven while still on earth!

The prophetic voice of Ruth Heflin led many to a deeper understanding of praise, worship, and glory. She wrote, "What is the glory realm? It is the realm of eternity. It is the revelation of the presence of God. It is the manifestation of His presence. He is glory. He is everywhere, but glory is the manifestation of that reality. Earth has the atmosphere of air, whereas the heavenly atmosphere is glory, His presence. When glory comes down, it's a bit of Heaven's atmosphere coming down to us, a taste of His manifest presence." [6]

In modern Christianity, we have heard much talk about the original sin that caused the severe and deadly break in our relationship with our Creator. As surely as the lack of breath in our lungs causes death to the body, the separation from God's glory brought death to our human spirit. We know that Christ, our Messiah, Himself paid the price for reconciliation to restore the broken relationship. But forgiveness of the original sin is not the end goal of Christ's sacrificial gift. Neither is it merely the obtaining of a future in Heaven for individual comfort.

> **The real accomplishment of the cross was restoration to the opportunity to abide in His original glory. Now.**

The real accomplishment of the cross was restoration to the opportunity to abide in His original glory. Now.

To breathe in the air of Heaven as surely as we breathe the air of Earth. This is what Jesus modeled and made possible for us. Scripture explains that this divine purpose and destiny of abiding in the glory is the ultimate goal of the human journey. It also provides understanding on how our prayers can shift from human centered pleas to God centered proclamations.

> *"For those He foreknew He also predestined to be conformed to the image of His Son, so that He would be the firstborn among many brothers. And those He predestined, He also called; and those He called, He also justified; and those He justified, He also glorified." Romans 8:29-30*

Each of these words reflect a stage in our spiritual journey that restores the identity we were created to express. While many scholars have expounded upon this powerful passage, the insights of Robert Henderson have had significant impact on my understanding of prayer that moves from groans to glory.[7]

"Foreknew" and **"Predestined"** communicate God's pre-existing knowledge of His plan to conform us to His image. Christ is the revelation of what it looks like to be a human created in His image. Our unique story and expression of becoming like Christ and a part of His body were written before we were born.

The fact that our story begins "predestined" does not negate the importance and gift of free will. We have a destiny written and known by Creator, but our choices and responses impact the timing, degree, and emotions we experience on the journey. I believe personal intimacy and obedience, coupled with intercession by and for others have huge impact on fulfilling destiny.

"Called" indicates God's communication of that pre-known and planned story to us. We begin to seek and know what our calling is. Aptitude, skill, and gifting often influence and shape calling. There is communication and conversation between Creator and creation during this stage. Discovery of purpose and meaning in our individual lives aligns with divine appointments and connections.

The role of blessings, gifting, and callings in the past family line has present influence. Past agreements and actions of previous generations can both positively and negatively affect our present calling and destiny. Because God is eternal and our human spirit transcends our limited physical body, the impact of this truth will be examined and explored in a future chapter.

"Justified" describes the act of being changed and restored to a relationship with God that allows us to be able to fulfill the calling. The legal transaction was completed at the cross. The exchange was our sin for His righteousness. Now the process of walking out the new life is possible through the exchange that involves removing any thing- attitude, action or thought- that does not conform to the image of Christ. The tools that God often uses in this process are trials, testing and suffering.

Then, as a final destination, we are "**Glorified.**" In this incredible stage, The Almighty One, The Ancient of Days, invites us to carry His glory! Because we are in Christ and Christ is in us, we can breathe the atmosphere of Heaven. As we mature into the calling and destiny prepared for us, we exercise authority in our sphere of influence. Our presence causes the atmosphere around us to change.

While some have interpreted this ultimate experience of glory as possible only in Heaven, after a physical death, I believe Scripture clearly declares this privilege and responsibility is for NOW. Gazing into His face, we are transformed into His image from glory to glory (2 Corinthians 3:18.) Christ has bridged and connected time and eternity. In His own words, He taught us to pray that the Kingdom of Heaven would come and God's will be done on EARTH as it already is in Heaven.

Perhaps most fascinating is that Christ is even now, presently declaring glory over us. He clarified that this prayer was, "...not only for these (disciples), but for those who believe in Me through their message." In John 17 He said,

"I have given them the glory You have given Me.
May they be one as We are one." John 17:22

Discovering our true identity, our calling to be conformed to His image, and learning to abide in His glory hold the secret to seeing Christ's model prayer fulfilled. Learning to offer effective intercession that carries His glory is how this Lord's prayer is multiplied beyond our individual lives to family, friends, cities, and nations, paving the way for His will to be done in the whole Earth.

Eternal God and Creator,

I stand in awe before Your Majesty. What a crazy yet marvelous idea that You would create me in Your image! I am so grateful for the invitation to converse with You and enter into Your presence. I realize my knowledge of Your glory and goodness is so limited, but the more I know, the more I love and adore You!

Thank You for the gift of life- a life known and a story written by You before I even existed. Thank You for my heritage and bloodline that enable me to fulfill the calling and purpose You prepared for me. Please remember the prayers of past generations and allow me to be a part of Your faithful answer to them.

I declare that my personal sin and those of generations past are paid for in full by the blood of Jesus Christ. His sacrifice justified me, and the enemy has no legal authority to hinder my destiny to be conformed to Christ. I receive and carry His glory in my human body. Amen.

Genesis 1:26, Psalm 33:11,16:6, Isaiah 53:5-6, 1 John 4:4

5

Now Eye See!

This is nothing short of phenomenal! You are created in the image of Almighty God. You are created with a capacity to breathe in God's glory and experience the atmosphere of heaven. You are invited into relationship with your loving Father. God knew you before creation, uniquely designed a body and a heritage to catalyze your destiny, and now invites your participation to see it to completion!

Are you beginning to "see" the hope of glory here on earth as it already is in Heaven, yet wondering why you are still not experiencing the reality of this wondrous possibility? Twenty-two years ago, God used a season of physical suffering to teach me a rich lesson on perspective.

Since our spirit is contained in a physical vessel, it requires intentional effort to "see" God's plans for ourselves and others from His perspective.

I vividly remember the sense of wonder that swept over me that day many years ago. I was somewhere between an awkward, slightly chubby sixth grader and a slimmer but overly self-conscious seventh grader. The idea of wearing the neat little, octagonal-shaped, wire-rimmed glasses did not excite me, especially since braces for my teeth were also soon forthcoming. But I quietly slipped them on in the doctor's office and glanced around.

> **Since our spirit is contained in a physical vessel, it requires intentional effort to "see" from God's perspective.**

My attention was immediately drawn to the window. I jumped up and stared outside. A lush, leafy tree vibrated with life as each individual leaf was brought into clear focus. The brilliant sunshine accentuated every crisp detail, contrasting endless hues of green. I couldn't believe my eyes and exclaimed in amazement, "Has everything always looked like this? Why has no one ever told me what I was missing?"

Anyone who wears correction for their physical eyesight can probably identify with this dramatic discovery. It is like discovering a whole new world filled with clarity, focus, facial expressions, and detail that was previously a hazy blur. Good vision is something we take for granted...until.

The date was March 1995. At a church ladies retreat, a lovely lady shared on the theme, "God's grace is sufficient," from 2 Corinthians 12:9. Though she was a devoted Christian mother who prayed daily for her children, God had allowed tragedy to invade their family. Her oldest daughter was almost killed in an auto accident, but by God's grace was now recuperating and re-learning how to live as a quadriplegic.

We marveled at this mother's sweet spirit as the story unfolded, and God's sovereignty, wisdom, and character were exalted through her testimony. That night, my roommates and I talked late into the night. And as women will, we covered almost every subject imaginable. As I fiddled with my contacts, solution, and case, one roommate mentioned she had undergone RK surgery (radial caratonomy) to correct near-sightedness and was extremely pleased with the results. I had thought about this surgery for years and decided to investigate it further as soon as I got home.

An evaluation the next Tuesday indicated I was a perfect candidate and the surgery was set for Friday. RK surgery involves making several radial (like spokes of a bicycle wheel) incisions to flatten the cornea of the eye, causing the light to refract more accurately on the retina, thereby improving vision without glasses or contacts. The surgery was to be performed with a "diamond edged knife."

I proceeded with the scheduled surgery, right eye on Friday with plans for the left eye on Monday. But by Saturday something seemed wrong. My vision was getting blurrier instead of clearer and the pain was intensifying. I called my doctor's emergency line on Sunday and he saw me early Monday morning. He looked very serious and said, "You definitely have an infection."

Without belaboring the details, the infection quickly infiltrated the corneal incision, and my vision deteriorated to the point I couldn't see my own hand in front of my face. After a week of antibiotic drops every few minutes, I was admitted to the hospital in an effort to gain control over the infection before it caused a corneal perforation, requiring an emergency corneal transplant. My family began to sense the seriousness of the infection, and we began asking for urgent prayer. The Body of Christ responded with a gracious outpouring of prayer, calls, and practical support.

After three days, I was released from the hospital. After several weeks, my vision gradually began to improve. Even now, 22 years later, scarring is present to remind me of the journey; although my sight is still poor in my right eye, the "good" eye has allowed me to return to a normal routine. What has been lost to physical sight, God more than restored in spiritual sight and understanding.

When God wants to secure the attention of an avid reader, one sure way is to take away eyesight. During those quiet moments in the hospital, relieved momentarily from the responsibility of caring for my four young children, I fellowshipped with my Lord in a unique way. Rather than reading and studying my beloved Bible, I could only meditate on that which was already hidden in my heart and listen as God wove the pieces together, bringing meaning and purpose from the pain and darkness.

God brought to my remembrance the story of how Christ healed a blind man. But the man opened his eyes, only to see "men as trees walking." Then Christ touched his eyes again and all things became clear. Soon after I returned from the hospital, a kind friend volunteered to come help me one afternoon. Knowing she would understand my hunger to hear from God concerning the relevance of this particular story, I asked her to read Mark 8.

One commentary (Jameison, Fauset, Brown) amplified Mark 8:25 by explaining, "Perhaps the one operation perfectly restored the eyes, while the other imparted immediately the faculty of using them. It is the only recorded example of a progressive cure and it certainly illustrates similar methods in the spiritual kingdom."

It definitely illuminated my understanding of acquiring spiritual vision. The doctors examined my eye almost daily. They explained that the eye itself, that is the retina, lens, nerves, and muscles were all perfectly healthy. The only reason I could not see was that my "window" or cornea was blurred with infectious infiltrates. The cornea which should be clear was swollen, red, and milky white. Although the "eye" behind my cornea was working perfectly, healthy and whole, the images I received through the cornea were blurred and distorted.

The spiritual truth stood out clearly. When I became a Christian, I was made perfect in God's sight, whole and complete. I was a new creation, restored to the privilege of an intimate relationship with God. Many verses confirm this regeneration: 2 Corinthians 5:17, Ephesians 5:26-27, Ephesians 2:5-6.

With these dramatic assurances of restoration and wholeness, why do we observe the children of God experiencing so much doubt, fear, and anxiety? Perhaps the answer involves how we "see" ourselves and our circumstances. If we are looking through a blurry, dirty window our images will be less than accurate. God's truth is the reality, but our perception of that truth is distorted by error in our thinking and the processing of information received into our mind. We "see" things from our limited, distorted perspective rather than "seeing" things from God's eternal, sovereign perspective.

While we are transformed from darkness to light in an instant (salvation), the transformation of our human mind is a process - a process that involves immersion in God's Word (the Bible) and an interactive prayer relationship with God. Like the blind man, our spiritual healing is in two parts. In the first step, our spirit is fully restored to a blameless, sinless, pre-fallen condition, an eternally secure fact made possible only by the substitutionary covenant of the Cross. His sinless life is credited to us! (2 Corinthians 5:21)

The second step is a "working out" of the transformed spirit in daily application. Like the blind man, we have a fully restored spirit, but also need to be given the ability to "use" or "apply" the change in our human bodies. This second stage of spiritual healing is what I compare to the clearing-up or healing of our spiritual "cornea", the window through which we view life.

Emotional and spiritual wounds increase vulnerability to distorted perspective.

If my eye had been "whole" and healthy, the strep-pnemo bacteria might have only caused mild annoyance. It was the presence of seven deep fresh incisions that allowed the bacteria to take over so quickly and thoroughly. The "wounds" made my eye extremely vulnerable to the destructive nature of a bacterial infection.

Likewise, emotional and spiritual wounds dramatically increase a person's vulnerability to the destruction of our enemy and distort accurate perspective.

It is a strong, healthy, spiritually whole person that can resist and overcome the evil one. In a fallen world, wounding is inevitable. That is why one of the primary ministries of Christ was healing. (Isaiah 61:1, Luke 4:18) Healing leads to a more accurate image of who God is, who we are in Him, and the truth about our circumstances.

Recall the passage from 2 Corinthians 4-5 in which the wholeness that occurs at salvation is described. Like the eye that was restored to the blind man at Bethesda, we become a new creature. The old things (wounded, fallen, and sinful) have passed away, and behold new things have come.

However, the "old things" seem very real and very much a part of our present lives. Several illustrations are given to help us comprehend this dichotomy. 2 Corinthians 4:7 says we have this treasure (light of the knowledge of the glory of God) in an earthen vessel (our body).

2 Corinthians 4:16 says our outer man is decaying, but our inner man is being renewed day by day. 2 Corinthians 5:2 indicates our "earthly tent" is groaning to be clothed with our dwelling from Heaven.

When we enter the place of intercession, there is a reality of how the situation looks from God's perspective. It is defined by the words He spoke and the promises He made. We must examine our hearts for wounds that would distort our view. We ask the Holy Spirit for revelation of wounds that have made the ones we are praying for vulnerable. It allows us to "see" who we are in Christ and renders the tactics of the enemy powerless to destroy that vision.

How we think, feel, and respond to God and others is a direct result of how we perceive the situation. If we see God as only a strict rule-keeper Who is angry when we fall short, we feel condemned and of little value. We drudge through life, defeated and discouraged. Our view becomes a functional reality even if it is not accurate truth.

Clarity and accuracy in sight develop in time spent with the original, with the person Who is Himself, Truth. Developing intimate relationship with the multifaceted, limitless person of God defines how we see daily life issues we are faced with. It changes how we pray, what we expect in answer to our prayers and intercession.

Perception determines whether we dwell in gloom or glory. It is essential to ask God to heal our eyes and allow us to see Him and who we are in Him more accurately. Believing His Truth turns mourning into dancing and fear into faith.

Precious Healer,

*You are Truth. All things were created by You
and for You. You define reality, and earth is
but a shadow created for Your purpose and
pleasure to reveal Your magnificence.*

*Jesus, I thank you that Your death and resurrection
have restored my broken relationship with a Holy
God. In humble gratitude, I acknowledge that
I have been restored to wholeness and am daily
maturing into a daughter who can experience
Your glory as I learn to abide in You.*

*I long to see life from Your perspective. I desire
to see people and land and government in light
of Your purpose and plan. I confess my wounded
heart has distorted my expectations and influenced
my actions. I am healed by Your wounds. Help me
to receive and live out that healing; blessing and
touching others with Your love. Please open my eyes
to see Your majesty, strength, power, and heart. Let
my prayers accurately align with what You have
declared over people and places and times. Amen.*

*Colossians 1:16, Galatians 2:20,
2 Corinthians 4-5, Hebrews 8:5*

6

Perfect

The presence of suffering on this planet is an undeniable fact. In an honest conversation about praying for people in need, we find ourselves asking how good could possibly come from such painful struggles. This book opened with a return to the garden where walking and talking with Creator was an everyday occurrence, and the glory of God not only filled the earth but was seen and known. Everything was... perfect.

The dramatic spiritual chasm that occurred in the garden resulted when Adam and Eve chose not to believe God and the Word He had spoken (that death would result from eating from the forbidden tree), choosing instead to breach the protective boundary He set by disobeying His command. When the "knowledge of evil" was added to the "knowledge of good", creation, which God had declared was "good" with each new day's project, became flawed and defective. Creation was no longer perfect. Relationship was broken.

One definition of "perfect" is "something completely free from faults or defects, or as close to such a condition as possible." Perfect used as an adjective can mean, "Having all the required or desired elements, qualities, or characteristics, as good as it is possible to be."

In Matthew 5:48, Christ commanded His followers, "Be perfect, therefore, as your Heavenly Father is perfect." This directive can cause a sense of hopelessness when perceived as an impossible standard. But understood in context as a process, it offers a key to understanding the role of suffering and trials that have resulted from the original sin and the hope of returning to the original glory.

Literally the verse reads, "Ye therefore shall be perfect," presenting the ideal future that implies an imperative. Consistent with Romans 8:29, we have a destiny to be conformed to Christ. "As your heavenly Father" implies the idea of unchanging, absolute moral perfection. In us the attainment implies growth, and the word is used of men of full age as contrasted with infants. In God, the perfection is not something attained, but exists eternally, but we draw near to it and become divine partakers of the divine nature when we love as He loves. [8]

The goal of being made perfect is best conveyed as the process of being shaped, trained, and matured into the being that is uniquely suited or prepared to fulfill our purpose and destiny. This gives new value to tests, trials, and even wounds. Suffering, whether a result of personal choices or inflicted by circumstances over which we have no control, can produce redemptive qualities.

In 2 Corinthians 12:9-10 a loving Father assures us,

> *"My grace is sufficient for you, for power is perfected in weakness." And Paul responds, "Therefore I will most gladly boast all the more about my weaknesses, so that Christ's power may reside in me. So because of Christ, I am pleased in weaknesses, in insults, in catastrophes, in persecutions, and in pressures. For when I am weak, then I am strong."*

The focus of much traditional prayer has been to petition God to remove pain and change circumstances based on what we think would be a more perfect situation. We expend much effort explaining to God how and what to do. When we begin to grasp that God uses all things to accomplish His purposes, it shifts the way we pray.

Christ is our perfect example. Though He was sinless and met the definition of being entirely without fault or defect, Scripture says He was perfected through suffering to accomplish His purpose.

*"Though a Son, He learned obedience through
what He suffered. After He was perfected,
He became the source of eternal salvation
to all who obey Him..." Hebrews 5:8-9*

The physical mind and body of Jesus, the parents He was entrusted to, and the time He was born were all uniquely designed for Him to fulfill His purpose as Messiah. The same truth applies to each of us. Our bodies, intellect, chemical balance, parents, choice of schools, and career and life experiences are also specially designed by our Creator to contain His "story" written for us.

It is easier to look backwards and see how God has used past trials to perfect us than it is to pray in the present moment for His purpose to be accomplished. For example, my oldest son has wanted to be a doctor since he was a child. As a youth, he excelled in academics and athletics.

After an exciting and successful season as a college athlete, he took the MCAT, applied to medical school, waited to hear results, and prayed. When the denial letter arrived, he was so disappointed. He felt in his heart that the medical profession was where God had called him. He quickly landed a job in pharmaceutical sales with high pay, perks, and benefits. One problem—he hated it. He wanted to be in conversation with patients, not customers. The experience reignited his passion for people and showed him the emptiness of money alone.

He resigned from the great job and took a part-time one in a physical therapist office with plans to re-apply to several medical schools.

This time he applied for early acceptance and was immediately accepted! The school he had chosen happened to also be the one a beautiful, godly, young lady had chosen; they fell in love and married as second year students! They graduate this year to begin serving God, being perfected into instruments of His healing, in the medical profession.

I am always on solid ground to ask that the enemy's evil intentions be turned around for good.

During his first denial, what if I had begged God to let him in that school? During the high paying career, what if I had prayed for him to be content and influence the business community? Neither of those prayers would have been consistent with the process God was using to perfect him for his calling as a doctor. God was developing humility and resolve. Praying from limited human perspective wastes hours of travail rather than walking in victorious worship and glory.

However, this doesn't mean every circumstance is good. It does mean that when I intercede for a prodigal child to return, an addict to be delivered, a financial disaster to turnaround, or for relationships to be reconciled, I am always on solid ground to ask that what our enemy intended for evil be turned around to accomplish good.

We were not only originally created in the image of God, but have a destiny to be restored and conformed to the image of Christ, perfected to become carriers of His glory.

We can declare with Paul that "The sufferings of this present time are not worth comparing with the glory that is going to be revealed to us." (Romans 8:18) Prevailing prayer facilitates the perfecting process. It moves us from worry to worship and from groans to glory.

Precious Lord,

I worship You as the Perfect One! You alone are flawless, sinless, absolutely pure, and righteous. You are the definition of Truth and Love. I am humbled that you would call me to be perfect even as You are perfect. I long to understand more fully what that means and how to obey.

You are well aware of the circumstances in my life right now. My heart is broken over my child who is struggling with self-respect and not feeling valued. Yet, my heart rejoices at the choices he is now making and the forward motions toward his destiny. I see you using his journey to prepare him to be a voice of hope for many others.

As I stand in the gap in prayer, I am also being perfected. You are teaching me to see the heart of a person from Your perspective, not outward physical limitations. Lord, use our voices to declare Your great worth! Continue to accomplish Your desire for my children and transform the thinking of this whole generation. May they see and know You! Amen.

2 Corinthians 12:9-10, Hebrews 5:8-10
Romans 8:28, Matthew 5:48

7

Earned Authority

Perfected through suffering- who else could create such an effective and diverse training program? Our loving Creator meets us at the most critical moment with Himself as the solution to our problems! The personal journey enlarges our heart, deepens our compassion, and clarifies our vision. It builds character, endurance, and even ultimately joy.

But memories of the dark and painful days are never too far below the surface. I remember the phone call like it was yesterday. Our oldest daughter was barely 21, and the years between high school graduation and this particular night had been tumultuous. Glassy eyes and oversleeping through college classes, late nights unsure where she was, overdrawn bank accounts and accumulating fees, more and more prescription drugs, and a totaled car in a one-person accident: all dangerous signs that I was just beginning to connect to a serious drug problem.

She had finally agreed to check herself into the local mental health hospital. They had stripped her of everything, even the drawstrings from her sweatpants. More constricting than relinquishing physical rights was yielding to their absolute authority. I was not allowed to contact her, and she was allowed only minimal and monitored phone calls.

Broken beyond anything I had ever known, I drove back to the hospital that night. I sat in the car in the parking lot, crying out to God for mercy. How could this child who had literally been prayed over every day of her life have fallen into such a desperate and life threatening place? Her father and I were happily married, very involved in each of our four children's lives, and very active in our local church. What had gone so wrong?

Just at that moment my cell phone rang. I would not have answered any other call, but it was my daughter. From inside the hospital she cried out to me, "Mom, I don't belong here. These people are crazy. Please get me out!" I had questioned myself in encouraging her to come here. Was this going to make things worse instead of better? Was she even safe? But the Holy Spirit took over, and I said, "Sweetheart, I am here. I am right outside your door. I cannot come in, but the Spirit of God had you call right now and led me to be right here, right now. He knows the pain that is wrenching both of our hearts. This wall may separate me from holding you physically, but nothing can separate us in spirit. The Holy Spirit will hold and protect you more surely than even I could. He is with us."

The recovery story did not end there. There were many more frightening and painful days. But our Deliverer prevailed! Our Redeemer continues to pour out faithful mercy every day! My precious daughter is now almost 7 years sober and happily married to a wonderful man she met in rehab the next year. God even blessed them with twin boys two years ago! My grandsons are surely a double portion blessing and a constant reminder of how our God turns mourning into dancing and groans into glory!

This journey of intercession as a mother of an addict has opened many doors to pray with other parents walking this painful road. I know how to identify with them in suffering like only one who has been there can. But it doesn't end there. I can also identify with the deliverance of prevailing prayer that brings hope that other parents may not yet be experiencing. I can share their present pain, but they can borrow from my present hope and make it their own even if they are not seeing it yet!

Personal prayer enables each of us to move individually toward our personal destiny of being conformed to the image of Christ. The process perfects us toward His purpose. Praying together with another person who shares the same burden adds power, confidence, and insight. We encourage one another, each adding a piece to the puzzle.

This power and boldness in coming before the throne to make an appeal for another person is possible because we have "earned" authority through our trials and experiences.

Power to make an appeal for another is possible because we have "earned" authority through trials.

The Righteous Judge always maintains law and order in His courtroom. The intercessor making an appeal on behalf of another presents the strongest case when they approach the Bench with "legal standing." A mother makes an appeal for her child or other family member, an employee makes an appeal for their boss, company, or industry, a recovered addict makes an appeal for another addict; all have legal standing to be heard.

Each person has a sphere of authority that God has established in their lives. It is usually tied to family, career, location in a city, or an interest or passion.

Sometimes a sphere of authority relates back to activities or covenants made by our ancestors. The family heritage influence involves both blessings and curses. The unique challenges and trials we face are often specific to our personal calling and destiny, and pressing through them to become more like Christ earns an authority that can be applied on behalf of others when we pray.

This makes logical sense to us when we have seen victory and have overcome through suffering, but what if in spite of surrender and obedience the result seems to be failure? Two specific personal examples illustrate this dichotomy.

Each person has a unique sphere of authority, usually tied to family, career, location or passion.

Four years ago, my family home place was at a turning point. Built in 1905, the well-preserved building where my great grandfather had lived and practiced community medicine had been converted to a restaurant and gift shop. When the people who rented the building broke their lease and left without proper notice, I asked God what to do. Through prayer, scriptural confirmation and counsel, I felt He was clearly leading me to open a coffee shop.

I dove in with all my energy, heart, and soul. For three years, I labored fervently without pay, learning to do payroll, licensing, marketing, media, inventory, and even some of the cooking (when I hate to cook). We hosted prayer groups, worship nights, small groups and networking. But I just couldn't make a profit. After three years God impressed on my spirit it was time to sell the business, lease the building, and move into another season. I was blessed by the many relationships that had been built and the new skills and insights learned, but the lack of financial success continued to haunt me and make me wonder why I had "failed."

Just into the first full year of the restaurant, a friend who was my Georgia state representative, made the decision to step down and run for a federal congressional seat. I had been active in civic roles and spent 10 years as a county planning commissioner. I had a heart for praying for political leaders and laws in our county, state, and nation, so when several state representatives contacted me about running for the open seat, I took the question to God. He reminded me of a word He had spoken from Zechariah 3 in 2000 at the beginning of the new millennium. I clearly heard His direction to run for the seat and fully expected to win. I did make it to a runoff against all odds, but I did not win the race. Again, I had responded to the call with surrender, sacrifice, and obedience, only to experience what surely felt like "failure."

Rees Howells, an intercessor who experienced unprecedented intimacy with God and authority in intercession, explained a revelation from his own experience. He tells of a consumptive woman for whom God had given him a promise and word concerning her healing. He had entered into such a place of agony and identification that he was willing even to take her place in death. God chose to offer him the opportunity to be a "living martyr" while calling her home after a season of believing and confident prayer.

Mr. Howells told of the Lord's dealing with him on this subject: "how the first-fruit-gained case had to go to the altar, because the first-fruits belong to God; and how, although the Holy Spirit witnessed in him that he had gained it, he had to walk it as a failure; and how through that the Lord gave such a sentence of death to the flesh, that in all future cases of healing self would take no glory." [9]

This concept brought fresh relevance to my experience of running for office and owning

> **Passion, often forged through struggles and trials, indicates where you are called to govern.**

a business. Both acts of obedience and sacrifice earned a place of identification and authority in intercession. Both were first-fruits placed on the altar as a sacrifice. Today, I pray for business owners and political leaders with effectiveness, power, and authority, and my sphere of intercessory influence has been enlarged. These apparent "failures" were used to perfect and prepare me for my destiny. Perhaps you can look at your "failures" through this new lens.

The unique passions, skills, and gifting you possess are an indicator of the sphere of influence in which God is preparing you to govern. But perhaps even more telling are the struggles and trials that God has allowed. John Hamill observes, "Through Christ, the struggle you and I are in the process of overcoming is actually forging within us the earned authority to set His people free. There's a question in the heavenlies right now that has everything to do with this crown and throne movement. Whose voice will prevail?... Thrones represent your seat of authority granted to you by covenant with Christ. Crowns represent your qualification to rule from the seat of authority He has granted you. In other words, they bear witness to your earned authority in the Spirit."

Hamill goes on to describe the scriptural model or foundation for this concept in Revelation 4 which depicts elders seated around God's throne. "These elders are the ones pictured in Revelation 5 with harps of worship and golden bowls of incense. The harp and bowl movement is patterned after the boundless worship and intercession of these elders. What's important to note here is that these elders actually have thrones, or governmental responsibility, related to their spheres. They minister to their spheres out of their earned authority which is represented by crowns." [10]

The ministry of intercession is for every believer. Unlike gifts or callings such as teacher, preacher, apostle, or prophet, intercession is a gift and responsibility rooted in the relationship to our God. The distinction that makes each person's role unique is the particular sphere of influence and preparation that an individual is given by their Creator. Governing from that "throne" allows every sphere to be covered: education, arts, media, business, family, church, and politics.

Recognizing where we have earned authority to govern also creates awareness when we are outside that sphere. There are two examples in Scripture when a person was not able to facilitate the answer to prayer desired. In Mark 9:29, the disciples asked why they could not cast the demon out of a boy, and Jesus answered that this type required prayer and fasting. In this case, they were missing the fervency and focus that fasting added to intercession.

In Acts 19:15, sons of a Jewish priest were attempting to cast the demon out of a boy, and it said, "Jesus and Paul I recognize--but who are you?" Clearly these men were operating outside their authority. Tragic backlash occurred. As we stand in the gap for others, it is crucial to operate with the level of fervency and intensity required, and to know and operate within the sphere of influence God has appointed.

King Jesus,

*You have been faithful to carry me through so
many trials and suffering. I am grateful for every
new revelation of Your grace and sufficiency
and Your presence in the midst of the difficult
situations. You have allowed me to overcome and
learn from these experiences and now stand in the
gap for others going through the same trials.*

*Christ, all authority is given to You! You were
perfected through Your suffering and have completed
Your earthly mission. I am seated in the Heavens
with You and possess authority to govern on
this earth through the power and revelation of
Your Spirit. I pray that every trial You allow be
transformed to strength for my effective intercession.*

*Lord, I pray that every believer will have their
eyes open to the eternal Kingdom purpose and
magnificent victory You have made it possible to
walk in. Reveal my sphere of influence and what
Your heart desires to accomplish there. Rebuke every
enemy that attempts to usurp Your throne. Amen.*

Ephesians 1:18-2:6, Revelation 5:10, Hebrews 5:8

8

Legal Standing

As we mature in faith, we become more comfortable and confident approaching God as Father. No longer perceiving ourselves as mere children, we linger in His presence, beginning to function as mature sons and daughters, exercising the authority He entrusts to us. No longer thinking like slaves, we approach Him as an honored and trusted Friend. The relationships as son or daughter and friend provide a strong foundation for intercession.

The most familiar instruction on prayer is the Lord's Prayer in Mathew 6:9-13. In this beautiful and classic example, Jesus is very clear that we are approaching God based on our relationship to Him as "our Father." Many books have been written on the rich depth of meaning and application in these few simple statements. In this model prayer, He moves us from worship to personal petition and corporate petition. He teaches us how to maintain right relationship to our Father through forgiveness and abide under His protection from our adversary. It concludes with a declaration of God's Kingdom sovereignty, His power to accomplish His intentions, and then attributes absolute glory to Him. Glory forever!

However, there is another less familiar example of prayer that Jesus felt was important enough to include in His teaching that prepared His disciples to fulfill His plans for them. It is the parable of the persistent woman in Luke 18:1-8:

> *"He then told them a parable on the need for them to pray always and not become discouraged: There was a judge in one town who didn't fear God or respect man. And a widow in that town kept coming to him, saying, 'Give me justice against my adversary.' For a while he was unwilling, but later he said to himself, 'Even though I don't fear God or respect man, yet because this widow keeps pestering me, I will give her justice, so she doesn't wear me out by her persistent coming.' Then the Lord said, 'Listen to what the unjust judge says. Will not God grant justice to His elect who cry out to Him day and night? Will He delay to help them? I tell you that He will swiftly*

grant them justice. Nevertheless, when the Son of Man comes, will He find that faith on earth?"

This remarkable parable introduces the invitation to appeal to God as Judge. The definition of intercession is the action of intervening on behalf of another. Synonyms include mediation and conciliation, terms often used in a courtroom environment. The Latin word "cedere" means "to go," so "go between" is the most literal meaning. In this story, Jesus praised the example of this woman's pleading. Plead is also a legal word, a formal statement by or on behalf of a defendant stating guilt or innocence in response to a charge, offering an allegation of fact or claiming that a point of law should apply.

> **The effective intercessor approaches the bench wielding authority based on the Judge's own words- Scripture!**

In teaching us how to intercede, Jesus encouraged us to appeal to the Righteous Judge to uphold His mandate of Justice.

The most effective intercessor approaches the bench from a position of legal standing or authority and a factual claim or case that is based on the Judge's own words.

Our Judge's words, decrees, and decisions are recorded in Scripture. The covenant of God, revealed in His Word is the foundation of any appeal to our Judge. That is why knowing and "praying-in" scripture is crucial. The finished work of Christ is the only acceptable evidence to present in the Heavenly Courts. Notice that in this example the woman did not deal directly with her adversary, rather trusted the Judge to uphold and enforce His decision and rebuke and restrain her enemy.

In the Old Testament, Daniel shares a powerful vision of Courtroom intercession. He describes seeing thrones set in place before God's presence with thousands upon thousands serving Him and standing before Him. Daniel observes that the court was convened and the books were opened. The courtroom scene escalates until in glorious finality Daniel says:

"As I was watching, this horn (our adversary) made war with the holy ones and was prevailing over them until the Ancient of Days arrived and a judgement was given in favor of the holy ones of the Most High, for the time had come, and the holy ones took possession of the kingdom." Daniel 7:21-22

In the New Testament, the book of Hebrews is filled with examples of legal terms and types such as covenant/ contract, decree/verdict, mediator, and hearing. It includes an explanation that our system of authority on earth is actually a copy or shadow of the reality in heaven.

"We have this kind of high priest, who sat down at the right hand of the throne of the Majesty in the

heavens... These serve as a copy and shadow of the heavenly things... For He said, "Be careful that you make everything according to the pattern that was shown to you on the mountain'. But Jesus has now obtained a superior ministry, and to that degree He is the mediator of a better covenant, which has been legally enacted on better promises." Hebrews 8:1,5-6

This is the foundation of the authority of our intercession. God is the Sovereign Law maker and Law keeper. Every concern, question, and issue we face in this life has a solution and plan that aligns with Creator's original purpose and intent. As we spend time understanding the nature and heart of God and ask Him to bring us into alignment with His heart, we learn to pray with power and confidence.

Just as important as persistence is knowing when to accept the verdict and move forward in victory.

Beloved, we are invited into this magnificent Courtroom by Jesus, the author and upholder of our New Covenant with the Father! He assures us of swift and timely judgment in our favor, asking but one question on which the results pivot, "Will He find that faith on earth?" Will we *believe* and act on the invitation?

Like the woman in the parable, intercessors must persist with a request until a verdict is rendered. This persistence is referred to as "praying through" to victory. There is travail and groaning in this action. It can take minutes, months, or years.

But just as important as knowing when to keep pressing in is the knowledge when to accept the verdict of the judge and walk forward in victory.

It would be unnecessary and even foolish to come back to the Judge with the same request after He had already made a decision in our favor. This would display distrust and unbelief in the authority and power of the Judge. The lack of faith and unbelief would thus prohibit the woman from entering a place of rest. After praying through a burden and receiving a verdict, I "rest" my case.

Righteous Judge,

We come before Your Magnificent and Holy Throne. You are Sovereign over all things, at all times, The Ancient of Days. We acknowledge that You honor Your covenant agreement forever and always keep Your Word.

Lord, we and our forefathers have sinned and fallen short of Your glory. We have sometimes, whether unknowingly or intentionally, allowed our adversary an open door into our lives. We desire to break any false agreement and close those doors. We repent and confess that You alone are our God. You alone are righteous, holy, and worthy of praise.

Christ, our Messiah, has paid the price in full for restoration of relationship with You. Satan has no legal authority because the blood of Jesus satisfied Your requirement. Would You now render a verdict in our favor in this specific situation so that Your Kingdom purpose may be fulfilled? Show us how to walk forward in the destiny and authority You have prepared for Your people. Amen.

Daniel 7:22, Hebrews 8:7-12, Luke 18, 1-8

9

Enter into Rest

Atlanta traffic. What a great time to think, talk, and pray. To pass the hour-long commute from my home in north Atlanta to downtown, I decided to call and check in with Susan. We had been playing phone tag, and I was anxious to hear more about the exciting update she had posted in her recent newsletter.

Susan and her husband founded Navigate Recovery Gwinnett, an innovative concept of networking resources and support for families dealing with addiction. Since God had allowed me to walk through this dark experience and see deliverance in my own family, I had eagerly supported her vision and ministry.

Susan bubbled with excitement as she shared how the new year had been met with unexpected favor and grace. A large foundation had offered to come along side NRG and fund a program for crisis counselors at the hospital. An open door was evident at the other local hospital. Years of sowing and sharing were beginning to blossom into fruitful harvest! I rejoiced with her while apologizing for not being more available for "hands-on" assistance. She knew I had been praying but I lamented that I had missed meetings and events. Susan assured me that our team of intercessors had been a key part of the present success.

I rolled up to my lunch appointment at the Municipal City Market. Oh, how wonderful to be out and about again after spending the first month of the year in hospital and nursing home rooms and recovering from my own minor surgery. I felt like my new year had just begun. Shealeta had quickly become a special friend since the day we met. As director of a large pro-life pregnancy center in downtown Atlanta, she had been invited to lead in prayer at the annual Right to Life Memorial Walk two years ago. Held every January 22 at the Georgia Capitol, I had participated most years in the service and silent memorial walk through the city.

That day, like many before it, was frigidly cold. The music and program had been inspirational. As the faithful crowd huddled for the closing prayer before the Memorial Walk, Shealeta stepped up to pray. And pray she did! As she opened her mouth, she began repenting for this tragic sin that had Atlanta and America in its evil grip, and declaring life for the unborn and mercy for all those involved. The heavens seemed to open and the presence of God filled the plaza. She spoke with an earned authority, grace, and power. The atmosphere shifted and it seemed heavenly messengers stood at attention. I knew I had to meet this mighty intercessor and beautiful woman of God.

I did follow that prompting, and every time we get together God uses our time to encourage and strengthen one other. Today would be no different. As we sat down to savor some tasty authentic Jamaican cuisine, I shared my lament of feeling like January had been a blur of lost time. My "down time" had robbed me of the "hands-on" activity I loved to be a part of. "Girl," she said with a smile, stretching the one word out to a sentence for emphasis, "Listen to the truth Holy Spirit just showed me as I prepared for my Bible study."

In the garden, before work, there was relationship.

She passionately explained, "What God wants from us is obedience. It's not so much what you are doing or where you are, but whether you are walking in obedience. Before sin happened in the garden, work was not a painful labor. The "hands-on" you are lamenting is the task oriented work that Adam was cursed to endure. Before that work there was relationship. Adam and Eve walked with God in peaceful, restful bliss. Sometimes God gives us the down time, seemingly placing goals and work "on hold" to savor special moments with Him. Don't rush through the season of "being" with Him in search of "doing" tasks for Him. Your time "on hold" has value and purpose."

Wow, what a refreshing concept, especially for an intercessor. While I often remind myself that prayer is effective and powerful, the American work ethic still kicks in and says, yes, but "hands-on" labor is better. It is rewarding to see the fruit of efforts; physical tasks are often more readily measurable and verifiable. Shealeta took me right back to the garden again! Created in God's image, created for relationship, and created for original "work" that was a pleasure rather than pain. The ruling and stewarding of the earth originally flowed with timeless joy and delight.

The intercessor often straddles a continuum. When do we "persist" like the woman in the Luke parable and when do we "rest?" When do we make a declaration of finished work and when do we press-through spiritual obstacles, strongholds that squelch victory?

In John 6:28 the disciples asked Jesus, "What can we do to perform the **works** of God?" Or in my words, "What can I do for God that is hands-on?" They wanted to see the supernatural miracles and life transformation in their own ministries. Jesus replied, "This is the work of God:

that you **believe** in the One He has sent." This answer seems counterintuitive. How can believing be "work?" Can one really accomplish something without "doing" anything?

In the book of Hebrews, the Holy Spirit warns readers three times, "Today, if you hear His voice, do not harden your hearts as in the rebellion." He explains that for 40 years an entire generation provoked Him by not remembering His incredible intervention and applying that trust to present circumstances. Their rebellion was displayed in two specific places- striving and testing their God.

> **Rather than "hands-on" work, God often invites us to stand, rest and watch Him respond.**

In the first place, the children of Israel complained about a lack of water, and God responded by instructing Moses to strike a rock. (Exodus 17:1-7) This place was called Meribah, which means *striving*. In this case God gave Moses a solution that required he **"do"** something. In the second instance, there was again a crying out for water in a place called Massah, which means *testing*. (Numbers 20:1-13) This time God asked Moses to **"speak"** to the rock.

Rather than doing a work that was "hands-on," God invited Moses to declare the provision of the Lord, stand in a place of rest and confidence, and watch the Lord respond.

> *"Take the staff and assemble the community. You and your brother Aaron are to speak to the rock while they watch, and it will yield its water. Then Moses raised his hand and struck the rock twice with his staff, so that a great amount of water gushed out... But the LORD said to Moses and Aaron, 'Because you did not trust (believe) Me to show My holiness in the sight of the Israelites, you will not bring this assembly into the land I have given them...' and He showed His holiness to them." Numbers 20:7,11 -13*

Wow, what a consequence! This must have been really important to God. Here was a nation of God's people, completing a 40-year season of discipline, striving, and testing, on the verge of crossing over the Jordan into a land of promise and rest. The leaders, intercessors who stood in the gap to mediate between God and His people, had seen previous success with "doing" what God asked. They prayed for water, and the method God used to answer was to strike a rock.

But the second-time, God intended to answer in a way that revealed Himself not only as provider but would give the entire community a glimpse of His glory. He asked Moses to speak to the rock and trust that in the *declaration* God would show them His holiness. He wanted the intercessor, Moses, to believe and trust God not merely for provision but to have faith in His character, timing, and methods.

Today much of our prayer, both as individuals and in groups, is still offered from a place of striving. Our eyes are focused on an unmet physical need. They are legitimate needs; finances, friendships, health, career conflict, family tension, as well as basic needs like water. Sometimes God in His grace tells us what to "do," giving strategy or insight to the work that leads to answers.

But when the deeper solution involves a spiritual shift, in the individual heart or in the atmosphere of a community, the prayer God requires is a declaration.

He invites us to speak in agreement with His Word, stand firm in confidence and faith, and watch Him act. He will show His holiness, His glory on earth as it is in Heaven, when we declare and believe. Holy Spirit says, "Therefore while the promise remains of entering His rest, let us fear so that none of you should miss it." (Hebrews 4:1)

When the solution involves a spiritual shift, the prayer God desires is a declaration of agreement.

There is more power in the spoken word than we could imagine. The entire creation story is established by, "And God said..." Created in His image includes the formation of a mouth to speak, communicate, and declare what is so.

When Paul said in 2 Corinthians 4:13, "I believed, therefore I spoke," he was recalling the words of David in Psalm 116:10. David was thanking God for deliverance even when it was not yet seen. He said, "Return to your rest, my soul, for the Lord has been good to you." Like prayer, words have impact that supersede time. Rest is possible due to the eternal, unchangeable declaration of God Himself. We are invited to agree with His living Word.

Living Word,

You are the image of the invisible God, the firstborn over all creation. I stand amazed that all things including thrones, rulers, and authorities have been created through You and for You by Your own Word! Your plan is written in the books of Heaven, unfolding according to Your time, which You also created.

There is a finality to Your work that allows me to find rest for my soul. Thank You for the invitation and privilege to join You in the work You are doing here on earth. My desire is to hear clearly, perceive correctly, and obey fully. I want to walk in and complete the good works You have prepared for me.

Lord, forgive me for striving when You say to rest. I do believe, help my unbelief. I ask that my words be in agreement with Your words about who You are and who I am in You. As I intercede, reveal Your view of the circumstances so I can speak and declare truth. Amen.

Colossians 1:15, Ephesians2:10,
2 Corinthians 4:13, Psalm 116

10

Praying in Time into Eternity

The place of intercession is a sacred place. Simultaneously our physical bodies breathe oxygen into our lungs while our spirit breathes in the glory of heaven. It is the unique place where heaven meets earth and we return to the garden to converse with our Creator. Prayer transcends *time* as we know it on earth, allowing us to feed the *eternity*-shaped capacity in our spirit. The wise King Solomon observed,

> *"He has made everything appropriate in its time. He has put eternity in their hearts, but man cannot discover the work God has done from beginning to end... Whatever is, has already*

*been, and whatever will be, already is, God
repeats what has passed. Ecclesiastes 3:11,15*

Prayer that connects the activities of earth with the plans and purposes of heaven is both powerful and timeless.

As we pray through a situation or need, we can move beyond the "seen" circumstance and, through the insight of the Holy Spirit, declare the "unseen" reality.

This is not mere wishful thinking. This is the process of coming into agreement with plans and purposes of our Eternal God. The passage from Hebrews 4:4 reveals,

*"And yet His works have been finished since
the foundation of the world... And on the
seventh day God rested from all His works."*

I experienced a practical example of how believing this truth influences perspective. Our oldest son was a senior in college and played offensive lineman for his football team. During an intense game, we cheered for every touchdown and knockdown, while grimacing at every penalty and turnover, especially when his number was called out, unsure of how each play would affect the final score.

We can move beyond the "seen" circumstance and declare the "unseen" reality.

After a passionate, hard fought game, the solid victory was wildly celebrated! Since the game had been televised and my husband recorded it, I watched it again the next day. My anxiety over the penalties and turnovers was replaced with a confident joy because I knew we had "already finished" the game and won the victory! What if we lived life with the same confidence and joy, entering into the rest of believing the finished work of God?

There are two principles we must believe in order to experience this glory and confidence in our intercession: First, that God indeed foreknew the entirety of our human life, and second that He invites us into the process and somehow weaves our intercession into the master plan.

Psalm 139 is the most beautiful affirmation of God's pre-knowledge of our life and destiny. David writes,

> *"For it was You who created my inward parts;*
> *You knit me together in my mother's womb... Your*
> *eyes saw me when I was formless; all my days*
> *were written in Your book and planned before*
> *a single one of them began." Psalm 139:13,16*

God was observed as an Author by Daniel in his vision of the Courts of Heaven. He saw the Ancient of Days open the books He had written. Jesus is described as the Author and finisher of our faith. Evidence of the concept that God has written a plan for humanity is found in Hebrews 10:5-7, quoted from Psalm 40:6-8, where it is said of Jesus,

"You did not want sacrifice and offering, but you prepared a body for Me. You did not delight in whole burnt offerings and sin offerings. Then I said, 'See, I have come- it is written about Me in the volume of the scroll- to do Your will, O God!'"

These passages teach us that every created human being and even Christ Himself have a "story" or destiny composed and written by God. The Creator then prepares a body specially and uniquely designed to contain the story. The story is eternal and spiritual. The body that contains it is physical flesh and blood. When we pray into or intercede for a particular person, situation, or circumstance, we step into the story at a particular time, but the spiritual influences that affect change transcend time and touch past heritage and future destiny.

Because God is eternal, His perspective is clearly infinitely broader than ours. Deuteronomy 5 reveals that He is a jealous God, punishing the children for the fathers' sin to the third and fourth generations of those that hate Him but showing faithful love to a thousand generations of those who love Him and keep His commandments.

While not a popular concept to contemporary grace-loving believers, decisions, agreements, and activities of one generation have repercussions on future generations. Though we are individually responsible to confess and repent of personal sin, Scripture teaches that past iniquity in our bloodline can be a hindrance to experiencing the destiny written for us. On the positive side, generational blessings are also a powerful spiritual inheritance.

Because our knowledge is limited to our own life-span or perhaps stories of parents and grandparents, the Holy Spirit invites us to pray in the spirit, listening for revelation and insight from the eternal realm. Romans 8:26 explains,

> *"In the same way the Spirit also joins to help*
> *in our weakness, because we do not know what*
> *to pray for as we should, but the Spirit Himself*
> *intercedes for us with unspoken groanings. And*
> *He who searches the hearts knows the Spirit's*
> *mind-set, because He intercedes for the saints*
> *according to the will of God." Romans 8:26*

Christ instructs in Mathew 16:19, "I will give you the keys of the kingdom of heaven, and whatever you bind on earth is *already* bound in heaven, and whatever you loose on earth is *already* loosed in heaven." This followed a promise that He would build His Church and the forces of Hades would not overpower it. So, if the enemy has a counter-plan of destruction for humanity, we are assured that we have the tools and power to overcome that plan and release the plans and purposes of God that are already established!

Just as we learned that the term intercessor is a legal, courtroom term, these terms of "binding" and "loosing" also reflect the legal concept of upholding or enforcing an agreement. A lawyer might interpret this passage to say, "Where a binding contract already exists, you have the legal right to act on it. Where freedom from a contract already exists, you are not bound to abide by it." It is extremely significant that the praying believer know and use these "keys" to facilitate the answer to His prayer modeled to the disciples, "Thy kingdom come on Earth as it (already) is in Heaven."

The "contract" that applies in our prayer is the Word of God. It is eternally relevant. Scriptural promises and His names and attributes are powerful evidence presented before the Throne of Grace. The final and living Word is Christ Himself; ultimately it is the blood of Jesus and His finished work of the cross that covers all iniquities past and sins present.

Eternal Father,

How amazing that You created us as spiritual beings, contained in a physical body for a season of time. Forgive us for spending so much more of our conversation in prayer on the needs and comforts of the body rather than spirit development. We desire to bring You pleasure, worshiping You in spirit and truth, praying in the Spirit.

Thank you for the gift of time. Teach us to number our days to accomplish the good work and Kingdom assignments You have prepared for us. Time is a tool at Your service, not a hindrance. Nothing is impossible for You!

Christ, You are the author and finisher of my faith. What issues am I praying for that are already settled in Heaven, and I need to move from pleading to proclamation? You are Lord of Angel Armies, and I ask You to dispense these eternal spirits to assist in the accomplishment of Your earthly purpose today. Enlarge my faith and do what only You can do! I lay down human effort and trust in You. Amen.

Psalm 90:12, John 4:24, Romans 8:26
Psalm 139, Psalm 91:11

11

Abiding in Christ

Her head was bowed but her eyes looked up at me. "Teresa, I never know if you are talking or praying!" We both laughed. Debi had been a God-sent answer to me at the café. Her love of cooking filled the gaping hole in my ability to fulfill the call to own and run a restaurant as God had led me to do. This was one of the many times our discussion about the need of a customer, family member, or friend slid easily from conversation to intercession.

Each morning of the café season, I would acknowledge it was His business, invite His presence and leadership, and then abide in that presence while we worked. Jesus spent significant time and words to explain to His disciples just how critical this concept of abiding was to fulfilling the call and purpose He had for them.

Just as conversations between earthly friends and our heavenly Friend flow freely, there is only a fine line between talking and praying. Awareness of His constant presence is one way we can "pray without ceasing" as instructed in the Word. The fullness of the solution is discovered in learning what it means to "abide." Jesus instructs us,

> *"Remain (abide) in Me, and I in you. Just as a branch is unable to produce fruit by itself unless it remains (abides) on the vine, so neither can you unless you remain in Me. I am the vine; you are the branches. The one who remains (abides) in Me and I in him produces much fruit because you can do nothing without me." John 15:4-5*

This passage expounds on the critical, life-sustaining nature of abiding. In verse seven of this passage, Christ promises that if we remain in Him and His Words remain in us, then we can ask whatever we want and it will be done for us- almost as if He was the one asking. The fruit or result of abiding is effective answered prayer! He adds in verse eight, "My Father is glorified by this!"

The end goal of intentional, prevailing prayer is to experience the manifest glory of the Father.

Praying through to the glory is to pray past the present circumstances, on towards the accomplishment of the purposes and plans designed by Creator.

The word "abide" is translated from the Greek word "meno," meaning "remain or stay." It is used over 40 times in John and has a great depth of meaning and application. It can mean just to stay where you are physically. It also means to continue living, even under adversity, to keep

> **The end goal of intentional, prevailing prayer is to experience the manifest glory of the Father.**

on pressing on. It can also mean to not change, to stay strong in one's resolve, remain in common purpose with others.

There is also a sense that "abide" means not just to continue to exist but to continue to exist under adversity unchanged - not knowing when or if circumstances will ever change but not letting the exterior circumstances change or touch you. [11]

Not letting the exterior circumstances change or touch you! This concept of abiding is key to powerful, effective, overcoming intercession. When we are "in Christ" and He is "in us," we can be physically present in a circumstance, yet also present in the eternal, finished work God has already written. In His Spirit, the separation of the secular and spiritual and between earth and heaven is removed.

Praying directly with a person creates a strong sense of identification and the desire to share a burden. Often our prayer on behalf of another is done face-to-face. However, much of the work of intercession is done in our "closet." The invitation to intervene in a quiet place alone with God on someone else's behalf brings a new dimension.

Rees Howells found the Lord asking him to reach people by way of the Throne without always using personal influence. He began to see that according to John 15:7, asking and seeing answers would depend on his ability to abide. Because this "abiding" was to take such a central place in his future life of intercession, he often spoke of "guarding his place of abiding." [12]

"The way Mr. Howells maintained this abiding was by spending a set time of waiting upon God every day during the period in which the intercession lasted. The Holy Spirit would then speak to him through the Word, revealing any standard that he was to come up to..."[13] As the intercessor remains united to Him by abiding in Him, His power operates through the intercessor and accomplishes what needs to be done. [14]

How are you maintaining your "abiding"? I find that a journal is an essential tool. Each morning as I read Scripture, I write out specific prayers and promises.

The written Word therefore becomes the living Word, applicable and relevant in the present moment.

Even the passage that is traditionally used at funerals to comfort those during the loss of a loved one challenges our thought that truly abiding with Christ is reserved for after physical death. In John 14:2 Christ assures us He is going to prepare a "place" for us so that where He is, we can be also. This place to rest, remain, and abide has the same root word as the previous passage describing the vine.

> *"In My Father's house are many dwelling places; if not, I would have told you. I am going away to prepare a place for you. If I go away and prepare a place for you, I will come back and receive you to Myself, so that where I am you may be also." John 14:2-3*

Jesus is preparing a place for us to abide with Him. In verse 10 Christ uses a variation of the word "meno" again to explain that the Father Who "dwells in" Me does His works. Then in verse 16 Christ says that the Father will give us another Counselor, that He may "abide" or "be with" us forever. The Holy Spirit who "stays with" us and will be in us, opens the door to the Heavenly place, making it possible to transcend earth and be with Christ right now.

These passages set the stage for understanding a very intimate, ongoing relationship with God. Unlike a distant and superficial business relationship, Christ invites us to His family and assures us that we were not left as orphans when He transitioned from His physical body to His resurrected, spiritual one. It is from this place of unity, alignment, and agreement that He promises to answer:

"Whatever you ask in My name, I will do it so that the Father may be glorified in the Son. If you ask Me anything in My name, I will do it." John 14:13-14

I cannot fully explain why we do not always see the answers we seek. As we learn to abide, our sense of time and perspective align with His. Resting in Him, His Spirit flows through us, displacing anxiety or worry. We enter into His rest by belief. Our work and labor is simply to do the will of the One we adore. We are not pleading persistently to a disconnected God for His reluctant agreement. Instead, we become like-minded and mature as our tender Vinedresser brings forth beautiful, bountiful, "perfect" fruit.

Heavenly Gardener,

*I stand in awe and wonder that You have invited
me into a relationship of abiding in You. Truly,
You are the source of every breath within my
body. Your Spirit gives me life. I am dependent
on You for all that I have and all that I do.*

*Jesus, I want to be as perfectly united with You
as a vine is with its branches. Please give me
Your thoughts, priorities, and perspective on the
circumstances I am walking through. Whether I
am working in the marketplace, serving my family,
eating or exercising- I desire all of my activities to
be covered and surrounded by Your presence.*

*Make my prayers and intercession an extension
of Your heart and desires. Use time as Your
tool to accomplish what You have planned. And
please use my mouth, my hands, and my prayers
as Your tools as well. I believe every promise in
Your Word is true whether I see expected results
or not. Remove any hindrance in my life to the
fulfillment of Your miraculous intentions! Amen.*

John 14-15, 1 Thessalonians 5:17, Colossians 3:23

12

The Seed

Abiding in the vine is a strong, visual illustration of our relationship to God in intercession and ministry. Returning to the garden, another remarkable picture is that of a "seed." As we explore the truth of being created in God's image and maturing to be like Him, we see that our spiritual seed was contained in His body just as our human seed is contained within our ancestors from generations past.

The image of childbirth is such a powerful and relatable analogy. Truth on the physical level, the seen, brings rich understanding to the spiritual level, the unseen. From conception, the unborn child carries unique DNA, the unseen plan of a known future, unfolding as the baby grows day after day. Even in the womb, before we experience the multifaceted personality or physical attributes of our child, we pray for and talk to our preborn child. As a parent, we rejoice in every stage as destiny is revealed and experienced through growth and maturity.

You can imagine your tiny infant miraculously growing into an adult. While you do not have power or control to bring about the actual growth or development, you nurture, feed, comfort, teach, hold, support, and encourage your child at each new step. See now with spiritual eyes the spiritual seed within your child. They have a spiritual DNA, a destiny known in Heaven, yet unfolding through time on earth.

"Now the promises were spoken to Abraham and to his seed. He does not say 'and to seeds' as though referring to many, but 'and to your seed', referring to one, who is Christ." **Galatians 3:16**

Just as the potential for your physical life was held in the "seed" of your parents, grandparents, and generations before you existed, the DNA of your spiritual identity can be traced back to one seed: Christ. While yet unborn, we were "in Christ." This marvelous truth is the foundation of our understanding of how we can abide in Christ and pray with the authority and effectiveness that He showed us.

"He also raised us up with Him and seated us with Him in the heavens, in Christ Jesus,

*so that in the coming ages He might display
the immeasurable riches of His grace in His
kindness to us in Christ Jesus." Ephesians 2:6-7*

So now, take a fresh look at the situation you are praying for. While you may feel pain — as sharp and intense as labor pain — and grief over poor choices, lost opportunity, or shattered dreams, lift up your eyes and see that Christ's DNA has defined your destiny! Your spirit is developing according to His plan as surely as your physical DNA defines your body.

Just as you were not in control of the time and circumstances God ordained for your child's physical birth, neither can you create or force spiritual growth in a situation or in the soul and spirit of your child. There may be pain in the labor process, but lift up your eyes and see with joy the way God sees finished work He is forming!

The analogy of the seed reveals truth in many dimensions. When the disciples wondered why Jesus was not hungry, He explained:

*"My food is to do the will of Him who sent Me
and to finish His work," Jesus told them, "Don't
you say, 'There are still four more months, then
the harvest'? Listen to what I'm telling you: Open
your eyes and look at the fields, for they are ready
for harvest. The reaper is already receiving pay*

*and gathering fruit for eternal life, so the sower
and the reaper can rejoice together." John 4:34-36*

Jesus was well acquainted with agricultural seasons. What did He mean by "You say there are still four more months (future) but I say they are ready now (present)"? I believe He was encouraging them to lift up their eyes and see the promise of what the seed would become even in the midst of the process. His perspective is broader than chronological time -- it is eternal. He seemed to be exuberantly saying that although you may be the sower and see only the seed right now or a tender shoot, go ahead and walk in the joy of the harvest of mature fruit with the reaper.

He designed each seed with a future maturity and a promise of what it will become, and God is a promise keeper. Christ is the Lord of the Harvest and came to finish the work God gave Him.

*"Those who sow in tears will reap with shouts of
joy. Though one goes along weeping, carrying the
bag of seed, he will surely come back with shouts
of joy, carrying his sheaves." Psalm 126:5-6*

Friend, this is our destiny! By God's creative, marvelous plan and power, we are in a lifelong process of being conformed to the likeness of Christ. He is being formed in us! A young child can count on having basic needs met by a loving parent. But a mature young adult steps into a new realm: that of receiving inheritance. Unless our babies go through the sometimes-painful process of growing up, they will be stuck at the elementary level, never being able to receive the rich and bountiful inheritance that is theirs.

Breakthrough prayer involves seeing this incredible plan and promise of receiving an inheritance as a co-heir with Christ. It moves us past asking for only physical needs.

"Now I say that as long as the heir is a child,
he differs in no way from a slave, though he
is the owner of everything." Galatians 4:1

As heirs and intercessors, we have the same freedom, victory, power, and authority that have been given to Christ by the Father! God uses the labor pains, the trials, and crises to develop Christ in us. Graham Cooke speaks to the role of crises in this way:

> "Paul embraced his crisis situations: 'If we suffer, we shall also reign with Him' (2 Timothy 2:2) 'The Spirit Himself testifies with our spirit that we are children of God, and if children, heirs also, heirs of God and fellow heirs with Christ, if indeed we suffer with Him so that we may also be glorified with Him. For I consider that the sufferings of this present time are not worthy to be compared with the glory that is to be revealed to us. For the anxious longing of the creation waits eagerly for the revealing of the sons of God.' (Romans 8:16-19) This is not a revelatory experience for a future

time but a present exposure to the intentionality of God. We are living in eternity now. I have been experiencing eternal life in Christ since the day of salvation. On earth, as it is in Heaven. As He is, so are we. Greater miracles than His we will do. Eternity now! We are presently partaking of the divine nature." [15]

So, lift up your eyes, see the future destiny and purpose God has written over a present circumstance. In prayer, proclaim the promise of the future today. There will be times when we lament like Paul in Galatians 4:11:

> *"I am fearful for you, that perhaps my labor for you has been wasted."*

But as we labor in prayer for a child, business, city, or nation, we can be assured that our love and investment are not wasted. Embrace God's perspective and let it turn your weeping to joy as you celebrate our loving, magnificent Father, His Son, and His Spirit. God is an amazing mixture of unconditional love, sovereign power, and intentional purpose. We are invited to abide, remain, and stay in Him.

The genius of God's creation plan is that this eternal seed, the breath of eternal life and glory, is contained in an earthen vessel:

> *"Now we have this treasure in clay jars, so that this extraordinary power may be from God and*

not from us. Therefore, we do not give up; even though our outer person is being destroyed, our inner person is being renewed day by day. For our momentary light affliction is producing for us an absolutely incomparable eternal weight of glory." 2 Corinthians 4:7, 16-17

This is why we can pray through a painful situation to a place of overcoming victory. This is why we can act on and rely on the promises of an unseen reality before they are seen. This earthen container holds the most amazing treasure imaginable. As I abide in Christ, His Spirt abides in me.

Colossians 1:27 was my father's favorite verse. It declares that "Christ in you is the hope of glory!" As believers, we carry the very DNA of Christ within us. We have the ability and authority to change the atmosphere and carry His glory everywhere we go. Are you ready to step it up a notch and begin living on this higher plane? It is your inheritance as a son or daughter of the King!

Precious Lord,

What a treasure You held within Your earthly body. When You voluntarily stepped out of Heaven into the Earth Your very hands created, You carried the seed of new spiritual life for me and all mankind! The thought is too great for me to comprehend. Even then, You knew me and had a plan for me. I was crucified with You so that now I live by the same resurrection power that raised You up!

Faithful Father, You have been gracious to meet every need I have. I confess that I have been thinking like a child for too long. I ask You to continue using every circumstance, test, and trial to shape me into a mature daughter. The DNA you placed in me is an integral part of the Kingdom plan You have established, and I long to fulfill my role.

Please renew my inner person and help me keep my focus on the eternal priorities that matter most to You. May I see others as You see them and intercede accordingly. Amen.

Philippians 2:6-10, Galatians 2:20, 2 Corinthians 4:7-16, Galatians 3:16

13

Rise Up!

Atlanta, Georgia was abuzz with excitement as January 2017 dawned. Our young, sometimes unpredictable but beloved Falcon football team had steadily climbed up in the national ratings; by January 22 it was only one win away from a shot at the Super Bowl! The city was painted in red and black, and everyone greeted one another with the team slogan, "Rise Up!"

In a WSB TV article, Falcon players said, "'Rise Up'" isn't just a slogan, but about doing your best." "'Rise Up'" means you have to show up, you gotta show up then rise up," Vic Beasley said. "It's to play your best," Jonathan Babineaux echoed. Other players indicated the phrase was about more than what happened on the field. "That's coming together as a community, coming together as a team and rising up to the potential you have," Ben Garland said. [16]

Unknown to the rest of the City, a small band of fervent intercessors had already planned an afternoon of prayer for the City on the same afternoon as the historic game. Just blocks away, practically in the shadow of the stadium, 22 prayer warriors gathered on 1/22 to tackle a different kind of adversary.

The gathering culminated a week of prayer for uniting Christians across the world. Similar services were being held from Germany to Australia and in major cities in America. Earlier that week in Atlanta, believers gathered at the historic Ebenezer Church to pray for racial reconciliation and honor the dream of Martin Luther King. Prayer leaders gathered at the Georgia Capitol and prayed for governmental leaders and for the inauguration of our newly elected American President.

This small but powerful team of intercessors was pushing beyond personal needs and requests to stand in the gap for community, regional, and national concerns. As leaders of local ministries, each person brought with them a calling, anointing, and authority to shift the spiritual atmosphere in Atlanta. Like the Falcon team that was called to "Rise Up" to their potential, we united to rise up and overcome a spiritual challenge that required corporate, united agreement, and strategy.

Rising up as sons and daughters of the Sovereign King is the ultimate purpose and destiny for all believers. In this book, we have explored how to move beyond a place of pleading and groaning to a place of overcoming, victorious glory. It applies on a personal level and it applies on a corporate, community level.

The fullness of seeing God's Kingdom come here on earth as it is in Heaven will require the coordinated, healthy functioning of the entire body of Christ. Praying for breakthrough for an individual can be accomplished by an individual. But as we seek to see culture transformed and cities, regions, and nations changed, it requires the agreement of all the sons and daughters who have earned authority in those areas to unite in prayer. Each one of us carries a piece of the answer. United we cover a much broader jurisdiction.

There is great power in the synergy of united sons and daughters.

There is great power in the synergy of united sons and daughters! The unique gifting and calling of each individual complement and enhance the other. Throughout the years, traditional prayer and worship services have slipped into individual spectator meetings. When a Spirit-filled believer practices fervent God-focused prayer both in the closet and in the group gathering, expect fire!

Jon Hamill points out in his book, Crown and Throne, that as revolutionaries we are not called just to take ground from the enemy, but to govern with authority the land that is gained.

"Elijah's legacy is actually a prototype of the crown and throne ministry of today. We are called to be kings and priests- to minister to God and release His authority to establish His Kingdom. The secret to Elijah's power was simple but profound: He stood before the Lord. He learned the secret of entering the King's domain. Demonstrations of great authority came from his time before the face of God and standing in His council over the nation of Israel... That's how Jesus taught His disciples to pray. 'Thy kingdom come, Thy will be done on earth as it is in heaven.' Though many of us have recited the Lord's prayer since we were kids, most of us have interpreted the passage to mean that we should passively accept whatever comes in life as God's will. In reality, nothing could be farther from the truth. Jesus is saying that heaven is our plumb line for earth. It's up to us to hear and perceive heaven's desire, then bring this direction to bear upon our world." [17]

Not only humanity, but all of creation groans for the day that God's sons and daughters rise up and are revealed with the identity and authority God designed us for:

*"The Spirit Himself testifies together with our
spirit that we are God's children, and if children,
also heirs — heirs of God and co-heirs with
Christ — seeing that we suffer with Him so
that we may also be glorified with Him. For the
creation eagerly awaits with anticipation for
God's sons to be revealed." Romans 8:16-17,19*

Believers have an amazing opportunity and responsibility during our physical journey on this earth. We
are the gate, a uniquely designed connecting point
between heaven and earth. Paul explains it this way in
2 Corinthians 3:17-18.

*"Now the Lord is Spirit; and where the Spirit of
the Lord is, there is freedom. We all, with unveiled
faces, are reflecting the glory of the Lord and are
being transformed into the same image from glory
to glory; this is from the Lord who is the Spirit."*

As His sons and daughters, we carry and reflect His
glory. This glory, the manifest presence of the Sovereign
Living God, changes everything! We, His creation, shift
the atmosphere by our presence on the physical earth
and by our prayers that transcend the spiritual heavens.

I was recently invited to an "interfaith" breakfast to
collaborate with leaders from various faiths to solve the
cultural scourge of sex-trafficking. I anticipated there
would be differing opinions, but what I did not expect

was that the antichrist spirit and powers tied to idolatry would seek to dominate the room.

I spoke briefly to the one man I knew, with whom I had worked the year before organizing Christian unity prayer gatherings described in the first part of this chapter. I gingerly sat across from an elegant lady whose spirit I was drawn to. As we talked, I discovered she was on the front lines of a Christ-centered ministry that rescued ladies of the night from dark and dangerous circumstances.

As the meeting began, the first speaker, representing the Jewish faith, waxed poetically with quotes from Carl Sagan saying we are all made of "star-stuff" and that the "cosmos is within us." The next speaker intoned the value of her African spiritual heritage and led the group in a responsive ceremony where she called out various names of God, which she assured us were all different names for the same entity. She poured water on a plant and asked us to repeat an African word of agreement each time she called out a name. I was silent.

The next speaker identified herself as a Presbyterian pastor. She shared that many millennials flocked to her church, unlike mainstream church losses. She explained how they are searching for spirituality and finding it within themselves. There was no mention of Christ, rather positive energy, inner person discovery, and uncompromised acceptance of diversity.

By the time we broke for the workshop, the atmosphere was oppressive to my spirit. I felt false gods had been exalted and Christ sidelined for the sake of "unity." I reached across to my new friend and asked if we could quietly pray. Together we rebuked every idol that would raise its head above Christ and declared, "No King but Jesus!" We invited the Holy Spirit to take control, clean house, and shift the atmosphere so we could accomplish His Kingdom work today.

As we regrouped, the previous speakers slipped out, the Christian leader I knew stepped up and invited all to hold hands and pray before we continued. Unsure whether I wanted to hold hands in agreement or not, I joined the circle. Passionate fervent prayers and worship, exalting the name of Christ, began to ring out. The atmosphere shifted and Kingdom business commenced. Prayer changed the whole tone of the meeting and glory filled the room.

As we "Rise Up" and walk in this magnificent calling to become a generation of revolutionaries, we must realize that there is an ongoing spiritual battle for governance. True unity and synergy are found in worship of the One True God, Yahweh, through His son Christ and by His Holy Spirit.

Lord of Hosts,

How marvelous You are! Creation was made
by You and for You. Unbelief of Your Word
has caused brokenness that incites all the
earth to groan, awaiting restoration.

But You, Messiah, paid the price for that original
sin that led to separation and made restored
relationship possible again. Creation itself eagerly
watches and waits as Your sons and daughters
are revealed and step into our destiny.

You are a God of purpose and intentionality. You
are sovereign over all times and seasons. I am
grateful for this season in which You are uniting
Your People, beckoning Your Bride to intimacy and
empowering your Ekklesia to govern Your creation.

Lord of Hosts, awaken us as a mighty army,
trained and devoted to You. Holy Spirit, rise up
within us, shaping us into the image of Jesus, for
the glory of Your name and Kingdom. Amen.

John 1:3, Romans 8:18-28, Ecclesiastes 3, Luke 1:37

14

I am Certain!

The year 2017 certainly had its share of suffering and groaning. Personal surgery and my father's passing were only the beginning. A few months later my husband's mother would also join the saints in Heaven. That same month our son who had lost his job would press forward with a wedding overshadowed by uncertainly and concern.

Later in the year, we would encourage him and his new wife to accept our offer of professional treatment to deal with the overwhelming stress, anxiety, and fear that was fueling emotional breakdown and broken communication. As the adult daughter at home, I found myself immersed in helping my mother deal with the multi-faceted business and personal issues following her beloved husband's death.

God also began to reveal a new season for my husband and me. Our home, built in the middle of the family horse farm was now large and sprawling for our empty nest. We knew that eventual downsizing would involve selling the whole farm to a developer. Unsolicited, several companies began to pursue the purchase and development of our property. It marked the beginning of the end of a beautiful 20-year season of raising children and horses.

As 2018 approached, I came before my loving Father and said, "Lord, I really need to hear a word from You for this year. There is so much turmoil in the world. I am overwhelmed by both the opportunities and challenges in the new year before me. But more than anything, I want to hear Your voice, a *word* I can hold on to." It was December 27 so I resorted to a familiar habit and opened my Bible to Psalm 27. Verse 13 jumped off the page!

> *"I am certain that I will see the LORD's goodness in the land of the living. Wait for the LORD; be courageous and let your heart be strong. Wait for the LORD."*

There was my "word" for 2018! CERTAIN. It was only fitting after 50 years as a lover of Christ, seeing His faithfulness and favor year after year, that "certain" would be the word He spoke. Yes, I would walk in the confidence and assurance that He would continue to reveal more of Himself and release more of my destiny in the days to come. I wrote in my journal,

"Because I am certain of Your character, I am certain of Your promises and certain of Your faithfulness- I watch and wait. —NOT a passive waiting. A passionate waiting. On Your hilltop. In Your presence."

Waiting without the certainty of relationship can lead to nervousness, dread, and anxiety. But the context of this verse is that of a steadfast love. Imagine a young couple on Valentine's Day. The husband decides that instead of reservations at a restaurant, he will prepare a special candlelight dinner at home. When his wife gets home from work, he instructs her to wait outside a minute while he puts the finishing touches on his elaborate plan.

Waiting just outside the door, she smiles and thinks of what he is doing and how much she loves him. She remembers other tender moments, and the stress of the day melts away. Inside he is lighting candles, putting on their favorite music, and pulling a warm dish from the oven.

> **The waiting God calls us to is knowing He is always active on our behalf.**

This is the waiting God calls us to. One of knowing that He is active on our behalf, putting things in order. The delay is to accomplish the fullness and goodness of his plan. We know the capability and the heart of the One who told us to wait. Relationship defines the attitude of our waiting.

As I continued to meditate on my new "word" from Psalm 27, I moved from dwelling on "certain" to digging deeper into "goodness". This trail brought me right back to Genesis 1 when God declared every day's creation was "good." Over the next few days, I continued to meditate on certainty and goodness and while reading through Exodus was delighted to discover a connection between goodness and glory and waiting in His presence.

In Exodus 33:18, Moses asked to see God's glory. That is really the overriding quest of our relationship to God in prayer. We long to move past the pleading and groans of our human perspective to the eternal, higher God-perspective experienced in His presence and glory. God's answer to Moses was,

> *"I will cause all My goodness to pass in front*
> *of you, and I will proclaim the name Yahweh*
> *before you. I will be gracious to whom I will*
> *be gracious, and I will have compassion on*
> *whom I will have compassion." Exodus 33:19*

I was astounded that God had just personally promised me that I could be certain that I would see His goodness here on earth, in the land of the living. Now He was showing me that His goodness is such an essential aspect of who He is that when Moses asked to see His glory, God answered by showing His goodness! He actually interchanged the two words, accentuating both as essential to His character.

Years ago, in October of 1986, my spiritual journey catapulted to a new level of zeal and intimacy. After 10 years of personal bondage and struggles, a pastor and family friend shared the truth of spiritual warfare and overcoming prayer. At his suggestion, I opened the Word to Hosea, and it exploded with new life and vitality.

The passage that became my life verse in 1986 still vibrates with new meaning and application this year. Hosea illustrated the passionate love of God for His people through the story of a harlot redeemed:

"Come, let us return to the LORD. For He has torn us, but He will heal us; He has wounded us, but He will bandage us. He will revive us after two days; He will raise us up on the third day, that we may live before Him. So let us know, let us press on to know the LORD. His going forth is as certain as the dawn..." Hosea 6:1-3a (NASB)

This passage summarizes the whole heart and intent of this book. Our Beloved calls us to return to the relationship He created for us in the garden. It was very good. The wounding, struggles, and trials He allows have a redemptive purpose. Like a surgeon who "resets" a broken bone, the process brings healing. Brokenness moves to strength. Certainty comes from "knowing" the surgeon.

In every prayer, certainty comes from pressing on to "know" our God. Friend, I hope you have stuck with me through the sometimes hard to read theological foundations of this exciting truth. Eternal God and Creator invites us into a multi-dimensional relationship with Him as Father, Friend, King, Judge, Living Word, Spirit, Truth, Beloved Bridegroom, and so much more!

This relationship develops through a constant, fluid, two-way conversation called prayer. Who He is shapes our understanding of who we are in Him. It propels us into the destiny written for us and transforms the way we intercede.

It is my hope as you enter into your private place with God and dig into His rich and relevant Word, that you too will be CERTAIN of His goodness and see His glory! May your heart be encouraged and your Kingdom destiny released!

Almighty God,

Thank you for the certainty You give in the midst of an uncertain, ever changing world. You are the same yesterday, today, and forever! You are my rock and my fortress, my ever-present help in trouble and my defender.

In Christ, through the indwelling of Your Holy Spirit, all of who You are is available to transform all of who I am. My heart is lifted up as I wait in Your presence.

I agree with and declare every word of Psalm 24. Come, King of Glory and saturate my being, shift the atmosphere wherever I walk or pray, for Your name's sake. I speak blessing and favor over this generation and those to come.

You are strong and mighty. I put on the armor of God and stand firm, with every prayer and request, praying at all times in the Spirit, alert and interceding for all the saints. The battle is Yours, and the victory has been won. You are worthy! You are holy! You are my King! Amen.

Psalm 27:13, Ephesians 6:10-18, Psalm 24

Psalm 24
The King of Glory

The earth and everything in it,
the world and its inhabitants, belong to the LORD;
for He laid its foundation on the seas
and established it on the rivers.
Who may ascend the mountain of the LORD?
Who may stand in His holy place?
The one who has clean hands and a pure heart,
who has not set his mind on what is false,
and who has not sworn deceitfully.
He will receive blessing form the LORD, and
righteousness from the God of his salvation.
Such is the generation of those who seek Him,
who seek the face of the God of Jacob.
Lift up your heads, you gates!
Rise up, ancient doors!
Then the King of glory will come in.
Who is this King of glory?
The LORD, strong and mighty,
the LORD, mighty in battle.
Lift up your heads, you gates!
Rise up, ancient doors!
Then the King of glory will come in.
Who is He, this King of glory?
The LORD of Hosts, He is the King of glory.

Epilogue

As just over one year transpires since my sweet dad moved from earthly glory to heavenly glory, it is with great joy that I embark on the publishing of this memoir. The spiritual atmosphere has accelerated during the year with many specific instances of God's Kingdom principles at work. Having persevered for over 30 years as a prayer warrior, it is so exciting and rewarding to see more and more of the answers to prayers from years past.

In February 2018, I was blessed to attend a gathering of seasoned governmental intercessors in Washington, DC. Like many others, I sense that God is on the verge of hearing and responding to decades of prayers for a spiritual awakening in America. The conference was scheduled for 2/22, inspired by Isaiah 22:22, and was aptly called the "Turnaround" Conference. Dutch Sheets organized the event and invited many trusted prophetic voices. The event was in the historic post office, now a five star hotel owned by President Donald Trump.

The passage from Isaiah states, **"I will place the key of the House of David on his shoulder; what he opens, no one can close; what he closes, no one can open."** The original context was a transfer of power that took place in ancient Jerusalem in 700 BC, but as in many inspired passages, there is also a present application to the church today. The Greek word for church is actually "ekklesia" or a governing body. In the most dramatic fashion, America was in the midst of a tumultuous realignment to original founding principles, direction, and government, and the Church was prepared to take a stand and declare the authority of Jesus as our King.

One of the primary "giants" of evil that this Ekklesia decreed to take down was the tragedy of legal abortion in our country. Culminating years of prayer vigils, prayer walks, and activism, we declared that the Spirit of Life would reign, and a covenant of death would be annulled. We declared justice and righteousness over America.

In an unusual turn of events, the revered and respected Dr. Billy Graham was called to glory on February 21 at age 99. Numerous prophetic words during the last decade surfaced that indicated his homecoming marked a new era, a new season of God's mercy and outpouring of His Spirit.

I had heard Billy Graham's daughter, Anne Graham Lotz, share this very word herself at a conference about 8 years ago at the Cove in North Carolina. During the conference, she revealed that God had indicated to her that when her father was called home to heaven, it would mark a significant shift in spiritual seasons. It wasn't until after his death that she researched the significance of February 21 and found that is a day Jewish people read specific Scripture to remember and honor the death of Moses, the liberator of Israel. Anne felt like her father had been a Moses figure to our nation and that his passing signified a shift to the "Joshua generation" arising to lead the people of God into the next season.

As I shared in the dedication at the beginning of this book, God offered me personal comfort in the promise that as my own father was taken to Heaven, his "mantle" or calling and gifting would be passed on in double portion to his children and grandchildren. My father was like Elijah and his heirs like Elisha, building on a heritage of friendship with God and performing miracles that shifted and changed contemporary culture. I knew in my spirit that indeed we are living in a wonderful new day of God's intentional and intimate interaction with His people. As the most recent generation of saints, such as my father, mother-in-law, and Billy Graham were called home, their heirs would see Christ in a tangible and powerful way.

What is the practical application of entering into a "Moses to Joshua" or an "Elijah to Elisha" transition? It implies that we are moving from the initial liberation from the slavery of sin to a very real place of possessing the land or walking in the inheritance God has promised. Rather than salvation being interpreted as an insurance policy for life after death, it becomes a powerful, dynamic lifestyle of living and governing in alignment with Kingdom principles on earth.

Described as the "Last Days" in Joel 2, this generation is subjected to a very real spiritual battle. The dichotomy between government aligned with God's Kingdom and a global government opposed to God's ways and standards is raging through media and politics. Our enemy is still accusing and lying to humanity, but we, Kingdom sons and daughters, have greater weapons than ever before. This conflict and the promised victory were made remarkably evident in a situation with my youngest daughter.

On Monday after returning from the Turnaround Conference, I received a phone call from a woman I had prayed with several years ago. We shared a mutual friend with whom we had partnered in prayer during her marital difficulties. During those intimate prayer times, they had also supported me during my oldest daughter's darkest days of addiction and legal consequences. This call immediately turned serious as I heard the pain and fear in her voice.

Her beautiful daughter had attempted suicide the night before. An old boyfriend who rolled in and out of her life like a turbulent storm had evidently provoked the most recent bout of depression and despair. After taking over 50 pills from her parents' bathroom, she became frightened and called her mother. While racing home, my friend kept her daughter talking on the phone until she lost consciousness.

After arriving home, she performed CPR on her daughter's lifeless form; soon the paramedics arrived and took over. At the hospital, the daughter was connected to a ventilator and given emergency treatment. Against all odds, warmth and color began to return, and the next morning her eyes blinked open. God had saved her life! Clearly this child we had prayed for years ago still had a calling and purpose and destiny yet to be fulfilled!

Later that same afternoon, I shared the heartbreaking story with my youngest daughter, who is now a high school teacher in our community. She knows the family and their daughter, who was active in youth group activities. In fact, the best friend from high school of the young lady who had attempted suicide had led worship at a recent church discipleship retreat. We prayed together, and I declared over my daughter, "You will save lives. God has called you to do more than teach in your high school. You carry the presence, spirit, and glory of God into your classroom. You will save lives!"

She left home to work out at the local gym with a fellow teacher from her school. (The story of their friendship is a miracle itself. Not far into their first year of teaching together, my daughter and her new teacher friend discovered they had played together at age 4 at our previous church. Her mother and I also prayed together then and have been reunited to pray again now through our adult daughters!)

While working out at the gym, her friend shared that a student had come by her classroom earlier that morning. They began to talk, and the student confided that she had attempted suicide twice in previous years. When asked what had changed, she said that she had found God a year ago! Although she still struggled with depression, she now had help from God. Inspired by the Holy Spirit, this vibrant young teacher invited her student to pray over her classroom. What an example of earned authority and taking back ground from the enemy!

My daughter's eyes widened as she realized that out of the almost 4000 students at this large high school, this particular young lady was a student she had taught her first year. She was actually one of the students that she had prayed for by name, yet had no idea how God had intervened in her life. What an amazing confirmation of the power of specific, intentional prayer!

As my daughter excitedly shared this beautiful story, I helped her connect the dots. I had just prophesied over her that she would save lives. She had just been told a story of a student who had attempted suicide two years before; then God placed this child in her classroom and prompted her to pray for her by name. She did not know that God was already at work answering her prayers by bringing the student to salvation in Christ that brought literal salvation from death.

Although unseen, God was moving in response to her faithful service as a youth group leader and classroom teacher. Her grandfather's lifelong calling to teaching, evangelism, and prayer was being multiplied and poured out on her! We don't always get to see such a tangible answer to prayer but how delightful when we do glimpse His glory and answered generational prayers!

Two different stories. Two different sets of praying moms, 20 years ago and 10 years ago. A recent gathering of praying saints declaring a "turnaround" from death to life. And an eternal, almighty, loving God creatively intertwining intercession, answers, and destiny. Now, that's synergy of the ages seen in a new and vibrant expression!

I was touched on so many levels. The playful little girls we had prayed for over 20 years ago were now reconnected, praying together, studying the Bible, and teaching in public high school together—with lifesaving destinies unfolding! Ten years ago, a triplet of praying moms made a declaration of life over our children that perhaps foiled the scheme of the enemy who sought to kill and destroy but was not allowed to snatch a young life through suicide!

These are truly incredible days. My daughter's eyes have been opened to the imperceptible, ongoing work of God. Our God is making the unseen seen. The Ekklesia is uniting to declare this land belongs to King Jesus. His sons and daughters are rising up to govern in their spheres of influence and making a remarkable difference in our world.

My son whose story of brokenness opened the first chapter also continues to experience "turnaround." After wise counsel and treatment, his thinking has become more mature and responsible, and hope has been restored. God opened the door for a job that is uniquely aligned with his strengths. Just as God used Moses to command Pharaoh, "Let My people go!," and the children of Israel moved from slavery to freedom, my son is moving forward with each next right step. Like Joshua, he is seeing and believing, embarking on his unique journey to possess the land God has promised him.

Friends, look with your spirit eyes and rejoice! Ask God to open your eyes to see His perspective and watch expectantly. It is a process — one where delay, trials, and groaning lead to a glorious destiny. Don't stop too soon!

When He grants a glimpse of Himself, and you respond in love, worship, and obedience, you too will experience breakthrough in your prayers, and His glory and presence will rejuvenate your hope! May God abundantly bless your journey!

Endnotes

1   *Rees Howells Intercessor,* by Norman Grubb,
    Christian Literature Crusade, Netherlands,
    1952, page 86

2   Ibid. page 87

3   Ibid. page 89

4   *Glory, Experiencing the Atmosphere of Heaven,* by
    Ruth Ward Heflin, The McDougal Publishing
    Company, Hagerstown MD, 1990, page 79

5   *Prayer Portions,* 1991, Sylvia Gunter, Praise Page
    9,10. Used with permission pages 9 & 10 © 1991
    Prayer Portions by Sylvia Gunter, The Father's
    Business, P.O. Box 380333, Birmingham AL
    35238, http://www.thefathersbusiness.com

6   *Glory, Experiencing the Atmosphere of
    Heaven,* page 133

7   *Operating in the Courts of Heaven,* by Robert
    Henderson, Robert Henderson Ministries, 2014,
    pages 34-39

8   Ellicott's Commentary for English
    Readers via internet

9   *Rees Howells Intercessor*, page 104

10 *Crown and Throne*, Jon and Joleen Hamill, Burning
    Lamp Media and Publishing, 2013, pages 53-54

11 The Greek Geek: Abide-"Meno"
    www.blogos.org by S. Edgar

12 *Rees Howells Intercessor*, page 67

13 *Rees Howells Intercessor*, page 67

14 *Rees Howells Intercessor*, page 68

15 *Qualities of a Spiritual Warrior*, Graham Cooke,
    Brilliant Book House LLC, Vacaville,
    California, 2008, page 157-158

16 WSB TV Live article via internet January 31, 2017
    "Falcon players, fans share what 'Rise Up' means
    to them" by Tom Jones

17 *Crown and Throne*, Jon and Jolene Hamill,
    Burning Lamp Media and Publishing, 2013,
    page 28

Appendix

Maturing in Prayer: Public and Private

When I am asked how a person can move from routine, light prayer to powerful, effective, life-changing prayer, there is a two-part answer. First, **participate** and **practice** praying out loud with other believers. There is no better way to learn than by doing. Years of praying weekly with small "Moms In Prayer International" groups taught me to apply scriptural promises, listen to the Holy Spirit on what to pray, and agree with another person's prayer.

Corporate prayer and praying out loud may be uncomfortable for some at first. But there is synergy, power and completeness as each person adds their unique part to the whole prayer experience. There is strength and power in the spoken word. Many websites and ministries provide resources to assist in practicing specific, scriptural, targeted prayer:

- Nationaldayofprayer.org
- Ifapray.org (Intercessors for America)
- Momsinprayer.org
- Praygeorgia.com
- Jonandjolene.us
- Dutchsheets.org

The second strategy that adds depth and understanding to my prayer life is **journaling**. Since those early days in 1986, my love affair with Jesus has been chronicled by journaling almost every day. These are private love letters, written prayers, questions, and observations. It helps me to stay focused and see patterns. I write out my questions to God and record answers.

My special time alone with my best Friend starts with a cup of coffee early in the morning. (God loves coffee!) I write out a statement like, "Lord, what a beautiful new day You have made. I will rejoice and be glad in it!" I then read a Psalm and am usually amazed at how fresh and applicable the familiar words are. Often I see a note in the margin of my Bible from years ago and thank God for how He continues to show His faithfulness each new day. I may write a new note with today's date and a comment.

In addition to my habit of reading a Psalm each day, I usually read through an Old Testament passage and a

New Testament passage. While working on this book, my Old Testament reading was from Exodus. I also used the concordance to do word studies on concepts like good, glory, groaning, and certain.

Like David, the author of many Psalms, my journal is where I work through anxious or uneasy feelings to understand the root causes. I use bullet points from specific verses and words or phrases directly from God's Word to move me from questions to confidence. It is in this private and intimate time with my loving Father that the substance and confidence to move from groans to glory are established. My journal helps me move from a mere academic reading of Scripture to personal application.

Each person's journal will look different. I use capital letters, spaces, underlines and other design elements for emphasis. During Christmas 2017, I was missing my dad, Mike's mom and my son who was in recovery. Holidays can be tough and this one really was. Here is an unedited glimpse into my journal on December 29 of how I prayed into verses from Exodus 17 to move me from feeling sad and overwhelmed to experiencing "certainty:"

- "Is the Lord among us or not?" Your people are complaining and testing You in arrogance. Focus on the physical circumstances caused this questioning of Your character and presence. I pray for leaders to stand boldly on Your principles. (17:9)

- "Moses said to Joshua..." One generation speaks direction to the next- I pray for Your work in my adult children and my grandchildren. (17:9)
- "To the top of the hill..." Lord, teach me to see from Your perspective in the spirit, lifting my hands in intercession. (17:10)
- "Israel prevailed..." Lord, the battle is a process but Your purposes and plans prevail during daily intercession. (17:11)
- "supported his hands..." I am so thankful for friends who share the burden and the vision for victory. (17:12)
- "write this down. I will completely blot out..." Lord, I am believing You to completely blot out enemies of mental illness and addiction in our family. I am certain You can. (17:14)
- "built an altar..." Lord, I worship You! This battle is Yours and I declare Your authority and power over their careers, ministry and destinies. (17:15)
- "My hand is lifted toward the Lord's THRONE" I appeal to Heaven, my Righteous Judge, Sovereign of All to intervene on my behalf. (17:16)
- "The Lord will be at war with Amelek..." Lord, You are at war against every enemy intending to destroy my children. You are our defender and the war and the victory is Yours! (17:16)

These journal entries are just a sample of how we can apply and "pray-in" the promises of God. The more time we linger in His presence, abiding in the living Word, the more we mature into the destiny of becoming conformed to the image of Christ! The more consistent our thoughts are with the mind of Christ, the more we are transformed into His glory.

The next day was New Year's Eve. I was praying over my son's wife and decisions she had made. In Exodus 18 I was amazed that Moses was also interacting with his in-laws. After several verse by verse observations I noted:

> "Jethro (in-law) observed the present situation and came up with a God-inspired better plan so that, "You will certainly wear yourself out because the task is too heavy for you." Moses' Father-in-law said, "YOU CAN'T DO IT ALONE, NOW LISTEN TO ME, I WILL GIVE YOU SOME ADVICE."

While this story took place thousands of years ago, I applied it to our family's situation at that moment. I turned it into a prayer that after a time of separation, then intervention, there would again be a season of healthy independence. The relationships between husband, wife, family, and in-laws would all work together to accomplish God's plan in His time and in His way, to bring Him glory.

These are just a few examples of how personal and applicable the Word can be. To really experience effective prayer for others and experience the presence of God and His glory, we must spend intentional time in worship, reading, and responding. Intimate time alone with God is the foundation for effective, God-perspective intercession. Journaling is a great tool to chronicle the process.

As we saw in this book, God the Author has revealed His fabulous story through His Journal, the Bible. He has written a script for your days, your role in His story, from before the beginning of creation. As you turn each new page of your story, it will bless you to document the journey. His Journal expresses His heart and plans for you, your family, and your land. Your journal becomes an expression of your love and response to His love. Write on!

Reaching Higher

Conversation Starters for Small Group Study

I hope God has inspired you through this book so that you will want to continue to grow in your relationship with Him. Growth comes from searching, studying and being challenged by others. This section offers questions to gather with friends, families, or complete strangers to pursue the more God has for you in prayer.

You determine this size, location, and the frequency you meet for your gathering. One thing is certain- invite the Holy Spirit to your gathering and HE WILL COME! Your God desires to teach, inspire, counsel and transform your perspective. Enjoy His presence!

Chapter 1- I Will Pray for You!

1. What new insights did you gain from this chapter?

2. How do those insights change you and your prayer life?

3. Teresa shared the story of a loved one who was not experiencing the fullness of God's promises and seemed unable to overcome some very hard circumstances. Can you think of a person in your life that needs you to stand in the gap for them? Using scripture, list what you feel God desires for them, ask Him to show you hinderances to experiencing that desired place, then pray for God to intervene.

4. Why do you think a Sovereign God invites us to pray for one another? What changes can we expect when we pray?

5. Take a look at the Scriptures in this chapter and listed at the bottom of the prayer. How do they reveal God's heart for you and those whose life you impact?

6. Dig a little deeper into Ephesians 1:20-23. How does the fact that you, the church, are His body and contain the fullness of the One who fills all things in every way? Since all authority is under His feet and you are His body, specifically what issues will you take authority over today?

7. Read aloud the prayer written at the end of the chapter, then add your own words with names and specific situations the Holy Spirit brings to your mind.

Chapter 2- A Time to Groan

1. What new insights did you gain from this chapter?

2. How do those insights change you and your prayer life? How have these insights changed you view of intercession?

3. Rees Howells felt intercession must include identification, agony and authority. What areas in your life exhibit each of these? How are they shaping your prayer life?

4. This chapter asks the question, "How much of our groaning is over the loss of human comfort rather than grief over dishonoring God?" Ask the Holy Spirit to reveal the root cause of your groaning and invite Him to align your thoughts with His.

5. Take a look at the Scriptures in this chapter and listed at the bottom of the prayer. How do they reveal God's heart for you and those whose life you impact?

6. Dig a little deeper into Romans 3:9-26. If all have sinned and the result is falling short of the glory of God (verse 23), what is the path to return to experiencing His glory?

7. Read aloud the prayer written at the end of the chapter, then add your own words with names and specific situations the Holy Spirit brings to your mind.

Chapter 3- A Good Father

1. What new insights did you gain from this chapter?
2. How do those insights change you and your prayer life?
3. Genesis declares that you are made in the image of God! What does this mean to you? List qualities of God in one column and ways that you display those characteristics in a column next to it. Ask God to show you hinderances to displaying His image, then list the next specific step toward change.
4. How does the view of prayer as a relationship that is multifaceted affect your prayers? Make your own list to add to the chart on page 40.
5. Take a look at the Scriptures in this chapter and listed at the bottom of the prayer. How do they reveal God's heart for you and those whose life you impact?
6. Exodus 3:11-15 introduces God as "I AM". Then in John 8:58, Christ declares that before Abraham was, I AM. How do these verses transcend time? Search the surrounding verses and list examples, both old and new testament, of who God is.
7. Read aloud the prayer written at the end of the chapter, then add your own words with names and specific situations the Holy Spirit brings to your mind.

Chapter 4- Glory, The Atmosphere of Heaven

1. What new insights did you gain from this chapter?
2. How do those insights change you and your prayer life?
3. How would you define "glory?" Look up scriptures that contain the word glory in your concordance in the back of your Bible or on the internet. What do you learn from this word study?
4. Teresa describes the 5 words in Romans 8:29-30 as stages in a spiritual journey. How would you relate them to your own personal journey?
5. Take a look at the Scriptures in this chapter and listed at the bottom of the prayer. How do they reveal God's heart for you and those whose life you impact?
6. Dig in a little deeper into 2 Corinthians 3:18 using context, surrounding verses and commentaries. What is the image we are being transformed to? What is the difference between the glory we are moving from and the glory we are moving to?
7. Read aloud the prayer written at the end of the chapter, then add your own words with names and specific situations the Holy Spirit brings to your mind.

Chapter 5- Now Eye See!

1. What new insights did you gain from this chapter?

2. How do those insights change you and your prayer life?

3. Teresa shared the story of her eye surgery and how vision was impaired by a clouded cornea. Can you think of examples where your perspective has changed after walking through a trial? What aspects of God or yourself remained unchanged?

4. Read Mark 8:25 and compare it to other accounts of situations when Jesus healed people in response to their request. What are some present day examples in your life of Jesus using these different methods? Why might He choose different methods?

5. Take a look at the Scriptures in this chapter and listed at the bottom of the prayer. How do they reveal God's heart for you and those whose life you impact?

6. Read 2 Corinthians 4 with fresh eyes. Notice each time the word "image" or "glory" is mentioned. How is the glory that you carry (verse 6) a solution to the blinding of the minds of unbelievers (verse 3)?

7. Read aloud the prayer written at the end of the chapter, then add your own words with names and specific situations the Holy Spirit brings to your mind.

Chapter 6- Perfect

1. What new insights did you gain from this chapter?

2. How do those insights change you and your prayer life?

3. How would you define "perfect?" How does the instruction in Mathew 5:48 to, "Be perfect as I am perfect," make you feel? Building on the concepts from the last chapter, how does the process of being made whole and having correct vision restored relate to the process of being perfected?

4. List specific trials or hardships that you have experienced and how they have prepared or perfected you for His purpose in your life.

5. Take a look at the Scriptures in this chapter and listed at the bottom of the prayer. How do they reveal God's heart for you and those whose life you impact?

6. Look at the context of Matthew 5:48. Earlier in chapter 5 Jesus taught lessons from the sermon on the mount (verses 3-11) and just before this verse He compels us to love our enemies. How is loving like God related to being perfect or holy like God?

7. Read aloud the prayer written at the end of the chapter, then add your own words with names and specific situations the Holy Spirit brings to your mind.

Chapter 7- Earned Authority

1. What new insights did you gain from this chapter?
2. How do those insights change you and your prayer life?
3. The concept of a failure being used by God to establish authority in intercession is refreshing. Can you think of an example in your life where a sacrifice of obedience has been blessed by God, even if the outcome was not what you expected?
4. What is the sphere of influence God has placed you in? Ask Him what specific changes in those arenas He desires and has empowered/prepared you to accomplish.
5. Take a look at the Scriptures in this chapter and listed at the bottom of the prayer. How do they reveal God's heart for you and those whose life you impact?
6. Read the magnificent glimpse into Heaven shared by John in Revelation 5:8-14. Close your eyes, linger and imagine. Invite the Holy Spirit to expand your understanding of this throne room scene. What new meaning do the phrases prayers of the saints, worthy, redeemed, kingdom and priests to God and reigning on earth have to you?
7. Read aloud the prayer written at the end of the chapter, then add your own words with names and specific situations the Holy Spirit brings to your mind.

Chapter 8- Legal Standing

1. What new insights did you gain from this chapter?

2. How do those insights change you and your prayer life?

3. Share some examples where you have experienced the courtroom atmosphere. How is approaching God as "Judge" different from approaching Him as Father, Friend or Counselor?

4. Examine the requests you are most recently asking of God. Are there any instances where you are being persistent and asking repeatedly when there has already been a promise or decision/verdict made, and you need to move to praise and declaration? What is the difference?

5. Take a look at the Scriptures in this chapter and listed at the bottom of the prayer. How do they reveal God's heart for you and those whose life you impact?

6. The passage just before the parable of the judge in Luke 18 describes the coming of the kingdom (Luke 17:20-37.) List aspects of the Kingdom of God and how it relates to the teaching on prayer in Luke 18. How would you answer the question, "When the Son of Man comes, will he find that faith on earth?" (verse 8)

7. Read aloud the prayer written at the end of the chapter, then add your own words with names and specific situations the Holy Spirit brings to your mind.

Chapter 9- Enter Into Rest

1. What new insights did you gain from this chapter?

2. How do those insights change you and your prayer life?

3. How would you define "rest?" What are some synonyms for rest? Do a word study from your concordance or the internet on "rest." Use this insight to write out Hebrews 4:1 in your own words.

4. Give examples of times in your life when God has invited you to "be" rather than "do." What are reasons you tend to prefer one versus the other?

5. Take a look at the Scriptures in this chapter and listed at the bottom of the prayer. How do they reveal God's heart for you and those whose life you impact?

6. Meditate on Psalm 116. Verse 7 beckons us, "Return to your rest, my soul, fort the LORD has been good to you." How does the combination of God's goodness and our gratefulness transform an anxious heart?

7. Read aloud the prayer written at the end of the chapter, then add your own words with names and specific situations the Holy Spirit brings to your mind.

Chapter 10- Praying in Time into Eternity

1. What new insights did you gain from this chapter?

2. How do those insights change you and your prayer life?

3. Teresa shared the story of watching the replay of her son's football game and how different her emotions were when she already knew the outcome. Can you think of an example of something you are praying for that you would feel differently about if you knew the outcome? Ask God His desire for that situation and begin using the authority He has given you to declare agreement with His purposes. Ask Him to exchange His rest for your restlessness.

4. Psalm 139:16 reveals that every person has a story written and known by God before life begins. What are some specific and practical applications of this marvelous knowledge? How does believing this word alter your view of time and eternity?

5. Take a look at the Scriptures in this chapter and listed at the bottom of the prayer. How do they reveal God's heart for you and those whose life you impact?

6. In this chapter Mathew 16:19 provides a reminder that Jesus gives us keys to implement on earth the decisions, verdicts and plans that are established in heaven. Peter heard this teaching but did not yet understand it and Christ made the bold statement, "You are an offense to Me because you're not thinking about God's concerns, but man's." (verse 23) Is there

a situation in your life that offends Christ because you are not seeing it from His perspective and failing to use the tools he provided for you to manage the issue?

7. Read aloud the prayer written at the end of the chapter, then add your own words with names and specific situations the Holy Spirit brings to your mind.

Chapter 11- Abiding in Christ

1. What new insights did you gain from this chapter?

2. How do those insights change you and your prayer life?

3. Jesus used the example of a grape vine to help us understand what it means to abide or remain in Him. Can you think of any other examples or modern day parables to explain this truth?

4. Rees Howells found it essential to "guard his place of abiding." What can you do to guard your own place of abiding? Why is this so important?

5. Take a look at the Scriptures in this chapter and listed at the bottom of the prayer. How do they reveal God's heart for you and those whose life you impact?

6. Psalm 15 asks, "Who can abide in Your tent?" List the answers to that question David provides and ask the Holy Spirit to show you practical ways your thoughts and actions can be transformed to cultivate this place of abiding.

7. Read aloud the prayer written at the end of the chapter, then add your own words with names and specific situations the Holy Spirit brings to your mind.

Chapter 12- The Seed

1. What new insights did you gain from this chapter?
2. How do those insights change you and your prayer life?
3. Do a little internet research on DNA. What is the impact of the concept that we contain both a physical DNA from our parents and a spiritual DNA from Christ? Knowing that it is our destiny to be conformed to the image of Christ, how can you intercede differently for those you are praying for?
4. Explore the agricultural fact that a seed must die to bear fruit, and that multiplication takes place. How does this affect our prayer for a spiritual harvest? In an individual life? In a culture, city or nation?
5. Take a look at the Scriptures in this chapter and listed at the bottom of the prayer. How do they reveal God's heart for you and those whose life you impact?
6. Read Luke 8:4-15. In this parable Jesus compares the word of God to seed. Think outside the box a little. Does the "word/seed" abide in you? Do you abide, remain, stay in the "word/seed?" If all 4 seeds in the parable were the same "word", why did some mature and bear fruit and some did not? How does this apply to praying for the destiny or "spiritual seed" within someone to be cultivated and matured?
7. Read aloud the prayer written at the end of the chapter, then add your own words with names and specific situations the Holy Spirit brings to your mind.

Chapter 13- Rise Up!

1. What new insights did you gain from this chapter?

2. How do those insights change you and your prayer life?

3. In your opinion, how does the revelation and rising up of Kingdom sons and daughters relate to the earth and creation groaning? How does it connect back to the garden, creation and original purpose?

4. What is the importance of corporate or group prayer and intercession? How does what we have learned about approaching the throne of the Righteous Judge for personal needs apply to intercession for larger regional, cultural or corporate needs?

5. Take a look at the Scriptures in this chapter and listed at the bottom of the prayer. How do they reveal God's heart for you and those whose life you impact?

6. Ready for a real challenge? Try to memorize Romans 8! If that's too hard, read it over and over. This one chapter declares that the Holy Spirit and Christ Himself are partnering with us in intercession. No wonder verse 31 exclaims, "If God is for us, who is against us?" Take a moment to journal the impact this statement has on your present circumstances and future destiny.

7. Read aloud the prayer written at the end of the chapter, then add your own words with names and specific situations the Holy Spirit brings to your mind.

Chapter 14- I Am Certain

1. What new insights did you gain from this chapter?

2. How do those insights change you and your prayer life?

3. What attributes of God are you "certain" about? What new insight about your relationship with God, your personal destiny, or earned authority causes your prayers to be voiced with a new certainly? Make a list with two columns- one that says, "I do believe" and the other that says, "Help my unbelief." List both those things you are already certain of and those you want God to confirm with certainty.

4. Ask God to enliven a word from scripture especially for you, at the present time, for your present journey. Write it down. Say and pray it often.

5. Take a look at the Scriptures in this chapter and listed at the bottom of the prayer. How do they reveal God's heart for you and those whose life you impact?

6. Dig in a little deeper to Hosea 6:1-3. Is your Beloved calling you to return to a place of intimate relationship? Have you been wounded? Let Him heal you. For a fuller understanding of the restoration God offers to you, your family and your city, read the whole book of Hosea. Hosea 2:14-16 poetically promises that your valley of trouble can become your door of hope. Write out a prayer of receiving His offer to turn your groans into glory!

7. Read aloud the prayer written at the end of the chapter, then add your own words with names and specific situations the Holy Spirit brings to your mind.

P.O. Box 453

Powder Springs, Georgia 30127

www.entegritypublishing.com

info@entegritypublishing.com

770.727.6517

9 780999 178096